County Line

County Line

The Life Story of a
Minnesota Country School

By Peter Solem

Lulu Press

ISBN 978-1-387-54264-2

Acknowledgements

Writing a book was number one on my "bucket list" when I retired from a twenty-four year teaching career in 2013. I still had the family farm to care for, including a herd of registered Black Angus cattle, but I felt it was time to start doing a few other things in life that I had always wanted to accomplish. Authoring a book on local history was especially important to me because I thought it would be a lasting contribution to my community that could possibly extend far beyond my time on earth.

As I began, I soon became acutely aware of the large number of people I was dependent upon in order to complete the work. Fortunately, I found almost everyone to be extremely cooperative. I would like to take this opportunity to acknowledge their input and offer them a shared ownership of this book.

Completing *County Line* required an enormous amount of research. Countless hours were spent in the Auditor Offices of Marshall, Polk, Red Lake, and Pennington Counties laboriously poring through volumes and volumes of old commissioner books as well as an assortment of other documents. I want to give recognition to the staff members in each office for their assistance and incredible patience. Fewer hours were spent at the Recorder Offices in each county, but I also want to recognize their staffs.

Additional research was carried out at the District Service Center in Thief River Falls and at three area libraries: Thief River Falls Public Library in Thief River Falls, Red Lake Falls Public Library in Red Lake Falls, and Godel Memorial Library in Warren. The research at the District Service Center consisted mainly of reading old school board meeting minutes, whereas the research at the libraries consisted mainly of reading old newspapers on microfilm. I want to thank all of the staffs for their assistance.

The book in many ways was a family project. Everyone contributed including my wife, Valerie; two sons, Robert and Andrew; and daughter, Rebekah. Much of their involvement was with computer work, an area in which I badly lack skills. The fact that they all had considerably more computer savvy than I proved to be a godsend. They did, however, help in several other ways as well.

The bulk of Robert's involvement took place during the project's infancy. At the time, he was living on the farm at our family's log cabin, and he helped me get started by setting up a site on our home computer that was really convenient to use. Additionally, because I am able to type with only one finger, he did most of the typing throughout that early period. After Robert moved from the area, it was Andrew, residing just four miles away, who was frequently called upon for his exceptional computer knowledge.

Rebekah, meanwhile, is the family brain when it comes to knowing the fundamentals of writing; therefore, it was she whom I usually turned to with questions concerning grammar and editing. She is also adept at photography. The two pictures of me that appear on the back cover and About the Author were taken by Rebekah.

I am forever indebted to my beautiful wife, Valerie, whose encouragement and helping hand guided me all through the long process. Besides assisting me with the computer, she aided in many other ways as well. I can only imagine how many times she answered a question beginning with, "Which word sounds better?"

There were times when I realized that I needed counsel in overcoming certain roadblocks. I typically turned to Loiell Dyrud, a longtime friend and one of the smartest people I've ever met. He was able to spot my mistakes and omissions and offer valuable insights and suggestions.

The book's maps are the handiwork of Diane Michelle, a brilliant graphic designer who was a close childhood friend of my wife, Valerie. Thankfully, Diane was able to cope with my fastidiousness with detail, a condition exasperated by the fact that we were able to communicate only by mail and email. I am, however, thrilled with the results.

Proofreading a book's text is an extremely difficult and tedious task. I am grateful that Mandy Schuster, a good friend and former cohort from my teaching days, was willing to take it on. When she accepted, I wanted to throw my arms into the air and thank God that I was able to get an English teacher to cover up a social studies teacher's mistakes!

I am deeply indebted to Faye Auchenpaugh, an amazing and multitalented woman, who always seemed to provide me with assistance and encouragement when it was most needed. One such critical time occurred near the end of this undertaking.

The manuscript was basically finished, but I didn't have the know-how regarding formatting and other finishing touches. Fortunately, Faye accepted my plea for assistance.

I also want to give special recognition to Alice Hofstad. A retired library/media specialist from the local high school, Alice possessed the skills to improve and properly prepare the book for publication. Among the improvements, she greatly enhanced the book's photos and documents by rescanning the originals and making necessary corrections. It was Alice who helped me bring this nine-year-long project across the finish line.

Finally, I want to acknowledge the former students, as well as the former teacher, who shared their memories of County Line School either in writing or by interview. Their firsthand accounts in Chapter Five are not only enjoyable to read, they are also exceedingly informative. I owe each of you my heartfelt gratitude.

A Tribute to James Rude

James (Sonny) Rude was a student at County Line School from 1940-48.

While preparing a place to hold the spring picnic, his clothes accidentally caught on fire, and he was severely burned. Sonny was first taken to a hospital in Thief River Falls and later transferred to Gillette State Hospital in St. Paul, Minnesota. After a year-long battle, he died on June 1, 1949 at fourteen years of age.

At the time of the accident, Sonny had just finished the eighth grade and was very much looking forward to attending Lincoln High School in Thief River Falls. His surviving classmates remember his humor, cheerful disposition, kindness, and willingness to be of help. Sonny was well liked and respected by everyone who knew him.

Table of Contents

- Graduation Ceremonies
- School Picnics
- Other Events
- Conclusion

- Senora Swanson Almquist
- Marlene Kellberg Anderson
- Dorothy Muzzy Blodgett
- Muriel Copp
- Shirley Nelson Jasperson
- Emily Jacobson Johnson
- Rudy Rude
- Alfred Solem
- Roger Solem
- Stuart Solem
- Joyce Meyer Kron

- Annual Meetings
- School Funding
- Special Meetings
- Other

- World War I
- World War II
- Patriotism

- The Number of School Districts Soars
- Professional Educators and Farmers Clash Over School Reorganization
- Early Legislation
- Obstacles to Consolidation

Preface

This is the story of a school named County Line. It follows the life of a small one room country school that once touched the lives of an entire neighborhood in Northwest Minnesota. In fact, for six decades, nearly everyone who lived in this close-knit farming community was impacted by the school in one way or another. Not only did it provide an education for the children, it also served as the cultural center for the neighborhood.

County Line's story is similar to the stories of tens of thousands of rural schools that once existed throughout America. How they were organized and operated, the types of activities they hosted, and the impact they had on their communities were all very much alike. Although the primary focus of this book is on the County Line School, it is intended to be appreciated by anyone who has an interest in country schools.

My motives for writing this book have roots that go back to the 1980s. During that decade, many townships in my area were celebrating their centennials, in part by publishing centennial books of township stories and remembrances. Having been born and raised in Excel Township, I helped with their book that was published in 1984. We devoted a chapter to four country schools that had once operated within the township, but for some reason, County Line was omitted. It wasn't until years later that I began to question its exclusion. Why was this school left out when so many residents of Excel, including myself, had family members who once attended?

I eventually determined that the school's location was the reason: the County Line School District stretched across township lines, and during the greater part of its history, the schoolhouse was located in North Township, which was adjacent to Excel. We probably felt that North Township had a larger claim to the story.

Since the story was never written by either township, I decided to take on the project myself. I knew very little about the school, and my plans weren't very ambitious. An unexpected discovery, however, sparked more interest. While cleaning an upstairs storage area in my house, I came across a cardboard box full of musty smelling County Line records that had been left over from the days my parents had lived there. Browsing through them, I discovered that my mother had been the clerk on the school board at the time of the closing. Being the last clerk, it was logical that she would be the one to inherit all of the school documents. Much of the data found in this book comes from those recovered records.

As I began writing, I quickly realized how little I knew about rural schools. Three of my older brothers had attended County Line, but I had always been bused to city schools. This realization led me to broaden the scope of my writing. If I didn't know much about rural schools, I rationalized, chances were that few Americans did. The era of country schools had ended a long time before most of us living now were born.

I had an incredible number of questions for which I had no answers, and the nature of the questions seemed to change over time. At first they were mainly structural. How did a country school get started? How did it end? How did a consolidation of schools take place? How did the process of petitioning work?

As time went by, the questions became much more personal. What was it like attending a country school? In what activities did the students participate? Did they learn as much as those in city schools? Was the experience enjoyable?

Ultimately, I decided that all of the questions were important and that I should try a more comprehensive approach. I spent many months poring over volumes of records and reels of microfilm to collect as much factual information as possible. Perhaps more importantly, I spent nearly as much time visiting with past students, as well as the only surviving teacher, to get responses to my long list of personal questions. During the visits, I asked them individually if they would be willing to further contribute to the book by sharing their recollections either in writing or by interview. Consequently, the chapter entitled "Remembrances" is mainly a compilation of their efforts.

Because less emphasis was originally placed on record keeping, the data amassed in the appendix section of this book is incomplete. For example, there are no student and teacher or teacher contract lists prior to the 1908-09 school year, and there are several years of school board lists missing prior to the 1912-13 school year. If any reader can provide missing data, please contact me. In some cases, I have left blanks to fill in where information is missing.

It is my intent, however, for the book to be much more than a collection of County Line School data. I would also like it to serve as an educational tool for gaining greater understanding of, and deeper appreciation for, country schools in America.

Country schools are an integral part of our nation's history, and their legacy should be preserved. Finally, I want the book to be a source of enjoyment for everyone who reads it, but especially for those who attended the school, their families, and their future generations.

It is to the students of County Line School that I dedicate this book.

Peter Solem
February 2022

Prologue

A Public School System is Started in Minnesota

An education reform effort known as the common school movement took hold in America during the 1830s. Led by a Massachusetts' lawyer named Horace Mann, the movement clung to its core beliefs that education should be free, non-sectarian, and open to all school-age children. By the end of the nineteenth century, a system of publicly supported common schools was an important cornerstone to our nation's way of life.

The movement started in the Northeast and spread to the Midwest. When the Minnesota Territory was organized on March 3, 1849, Congress set apart two sections of land in each township to help finance a public school system. All of the proceeds derived from the lease or sale of land in either section sixteen or thirty-six of a township were to be placed into a self-sustaining school fund.[1]

On November 1, 1849, the territory's first legislative assembly passed a law to establish and maintain schools in the territory.[2] Its passage marked the beginning of the public school system in Minnesota. Among its provisions, the law established that any township with at least five families was to be a school district, a township with ten or more families could be divided into two or more districts, and the power to divide and form new districts would be given to the board of county commissioners.[3]

In 1851 the concept equating townships with school districts was set aside. A new territorial law was passed that required the county commissioners to "divide the inhabited portions of their county into convenient school districts."[4] If petitioned by a majority of legal voters, the commissioners could further "divide or alter a district."[5]

By December of 1856, the population of the Minnesota Territory had grown to more than one hundred and fifty thousand, and a bill was introduced to the United States Congress to allow the territory to proceed on a path to statehood. The next year, a state constitution was passed by territorial voters and sent to Congress for ratification. After considerable debate, on May 11, 1858, the eastern half of the Minnesota Territory was admitted to the United States as the State of Minnesota—the thirty-second state to join the Union.

Despite the change to statehood, the school system continued to function much like it had as a territory. Article 8, Section 1, of the Constitution of the State of Minnesota provided for a uniform system of public schools, while Section 2 provided for a perpetual school fund from the leasing or selling of school lands.[6] The way in which school districts were being organized, however, continued to change.

In 1861 the Minnesota State Legislature passed a law that established what was called the "township system." Each township was once again designated as a school district, and the township's board of supervisors became the district's ex officio officers. It became the responsibility of the town board to divide the district into convenient sub-districts and appoint a town superintendent to be in charge of the general management of schools.[7]

Finally, in 1862 the legislature settled on an organizational system known as the "neighborhood plan." This plan restored the responsibility of forming and altering school districts to the county commissioners and the right of petitioning to a majority of legal voters.[8] Only a handful of school districts existed at the time, but as the growing population spread to all parts of the state, it was the neighborhood plan that created thousands of new districts.

As part of the plan, neighborhood residents were required to draw up a petition accurately describing the proposed district and containing the signatures of a majority of legal voters living within its boundaries. It was then necessary for a spokesperson to bring the petition to the county auditor and request a hearing with the county board of commissioners. If granted, a date and time was set.

At the hearing, the commissioners listened to the arguments both for and against the proposal. Arguments in favor of a new school district usually described the lessened travel distance or ease of travel: parents didn't want their children walking long distances or going through thick forests and swamps. Arguments against a new school often described the harmful financial impact a new school would have on existing schools. Having fewer students meant there would be less government operating money available.

Before the petition could be approved by the county board, it needed to be signed by the county superintendent of schools. The superintendent was in charge of the general management of the county's schools and responsible for their well-being. The superintendent would determine how much harm, if any, a new district would inflict on an existing district and then decide whether or not to sign.

As Minnesota approached the twentieth century, there were approximately eight thousand school districts spread throughout the state.[9] The vast majority of these were rural and operated only one school, an elementary school for grades one through eight. These rural common schools were typically called "country schools," and they offered their students the basics: reading, writing, arithmetic, history, and geography. Most had only one instructor and held classes in small, one room buildings with no plumbing or electricity.

A Country School Named County Line

During the winter of 1894-95, the county commissioners of both Marshall[10] and Polk[11] Counties in Northwest Minnesota approved a petition by several landowners to create a new school district, District No. 72-219J. The school district would become known as the County Line School District, and its school would become known as the County Line School, or just "County Line." There was only one school in District No. 72-219J, and it conducted classes for grades one through eight.

The district was located a short distance northwest of Thief River Falls, a small, but booming, logging town. Uniquely situated, its location eventually involved four counties. The original school district was made up of parts of Marshall and Polk Counties. In 1896, however, Red Lake County was created from a portion of Polk, and County Line became part of Red Lake

County. Then, in 1910, Pennington County was created from a portion of Red Lake, and County Line became part of Pennington County. Consequently, County Line had the distinction of having been part of four counties: Marshall, Polk, Red Lake, and Pennington.

The district was also situated in a place where four townships converge. The Land Ordinance of 1785 had set up a method of establishing land maps and boundaries for land ownership known as the Public Land Survey System (PLSS). The PLSS divided land into units called sections and townships. A section is a unit of land that is one square mile in area (640 acres). A typical township is made up of thirty-six sections and is six miles square. The County Line District was created from sections in Norden and North Townships of Polk County and sections in Excel and New Solum Townships of Marshall County.

School District No. 72-219J was a joint school district. The 72 in its title was its Marshall County school district number; the 219 was the Polk County, Red Lake County, and Pennington County number; and the J meant that it was a joint district. Although the schoolhouse closed in 1949, School District No. 72-219J remained operational until 1955.

The district's size and shape changed noticeably over the years. It reached its greatest size in 1898 when the Red Lake County Board extended its southeastern boundary to the Thief River.[12]

School District No. 72-219J Including 1898 Addition

Map Year: 1898

6	5	4	3	2	1	6	5	4	3	2	1
7	8	9	10	11	12	7	8	9	10	11	12
18	17	16	15	14	13	18	17	16	15	14	13
19	20	21	22	23	24	19	20	21	22	23	24
30	29	28	27	26	25	30	29	28	27	26	25
31	32	33	34	35	36	31	32	33	34	35	36
6	5	4	3	2	1	6	5	4	3	2	1
7	8	9	10	11	12	7	8	9	10	11	12
18	17	16	15	14	13	18	17	16	15	14	13
19	20	21	22	23	24	19	20	21	22	23	24
30	29	28	27	26	25	30	29	28	27	26	25
31	32	33	34	35	36	31	32	33	34	35	36

MARSHALL COUNTY

New Solum Township · Excel Township · Norden Township · North Township

Thief River Falls

RED LAKE COUNTY

School District No. 72-219J (County Line)

Miles
0 1 2 3

In 1905 the formation of a new school district, North Star, took away almost one-fourth of County Line's land and drastically altered its appearance.[13] Having less of an impact were the occasional transfers of small tracts of land either into or out of the district by individual landowners.

The bulk of the district was sandwiched between two geographical features. Along the east side was the Thief River, which flowed south into the city of Thief River Falls where it merged with the Red Lake River. Near the west edge was a long sand ridge, once the shoreline of Lake Agassiz, a huge prehistoric lake. In between was the Thief River Prairie.

The original site of the schoolhouse is believed to have been in Excel Township and on the sand ridge. Its location changed in 1903 when the school district bought land in North Township and moved the schoolhouse eastward onto the open prairie. The prairie site was in a low, swampy area and when it rained, water was quick to stand. It was a condition that would plague the school for the remainder of its years.

At the time of the move, a one-mile grid system of roads marking the boundaries of sections had begun to take shape in the area, including a primitive dirt road just to the west of the school's new site. These roads were routinely used by students as they walked to and from school. They were also used by their families, often riding in horse-drawn carriages, as they gathered at the schoolhouse for special events.

In 1904 two railroad companies built tracks through the district: the Great Northern Railway[14] and the Soo Line Railroad.[15] The Great Northern Railway laid a track northward from Thief River Falls to Greenbush, Minnesota. It crossed the school district, following the section line that was one mile east of the school. Meanwhile, the Soo Line Railroad laid a track that was even closer. Their track traveled at a northwest angle out of Thief River Falls and passed the school approximately one-half mile to the east. The line then continued to Emerson, Manitoba.

In 1905 the Soo Line added "The Wheat Line" branch that went westward to Kenmare, North Dakota.[16] The branch veered off the trunk route about two miles north of Thief River Falls at a location that became known as Dakota Junction. On the way to Dakota, trains traveled less than three hundred yards to the south of the schoolhouse, the noise interrupting classes as they rumbled by.

In fewer than two years, three tracks had been built within a mile of the schoolhouse. Some of the students walked the tracks going to and from school. It provided them with a path that was free from mud and water. Needless to say, plenty of railroad stories surfaced during the following years.

The local residents viewed these neighborhood changes as progress and looked to the future with optimism. They realized that roads and railroads were an essential part of modern life, and they also understood the value of an education for their children. What they were yet to fully grasp, however, was the enormous impact the new school would make, not only on the lives of its students, but on the lives of everyone who lived in the neighborhood.

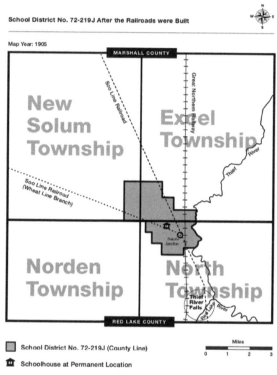

School District No. 72-219J After the Railroads were Built

Map Year: 1905

School District No. 72-219J (County Line)

Schoolhouse at Permanent Location

The following is the story of this remarkable country school.

1

The Birth of County Line School – District 72-219J

It was a pleasant August day in 2014. My elbow stuck out the open window as I slowly drove my old red Chevy pickup truck along a narrow minimum maintenance road. In the back seat, a spry, elderly woman, Senora Almquist, was anxiously anticipating her arrival to the site where she had attended County Line School as a young girl. Seventy-five years had passed since Senora had first enrolled, and she was wondering what she would now find. Her son, Bradley, a teacher from Kentucky, was seated next to her, and her husband, Basil, was in the front seat with me.

The one-room country schoolhouse had been located a short distance northwest of Thief River Falls, Minnesota, a prairie location marked by a nearby railroad track that ran westward to North Dakota. As we approached the track, I stopped the truck, and we climbed out onto the gravel road.

On both sides of the road were wheat fields, headed out, but not yet ripened for harvest. With little hesitation and what seemed to me few clues to go by, Senora turned and gazed at the exact location where the schoolhouse once stood. "This is it!" she cried out. "This is the right place. This is where I spent eight years of my life." She turned to the southeast, raised her right arm, and pointed her finger at a grove far off in the distance. "That is where I lived. I would come walking to school from that direction. I followed the tracks. Sometimes section men would come by in a trolley car and give me a ride." She glanced to the south where the tracks crossed the road about two hundred and seventy-five yards from us. "They let me off by the road."

Senora then turned to the west. Beyond the wheat fields stood a ridge stretching across the landscape from south to north, perhaps three-quarters of a mile away. "The Copp girls came from the ridge on a path along the fence line…over there." She slightly shifted her body to the northwest and continued. "The Rausches would be coming across that field." Then she pivoted some more until facing due north, the direction we had come from. "The three Solem boys followed the road. It was a dirt trail at that time."

As she continued to describe the children coming to school from all directions, it became apparent to me that her eyes no longer saw the wheat fields that surrounded us, but rather the faces of those whom she had once cared so deeply about.

Old Crossing Treaty of 1863

One hundred and fifty-one years before Senora's emotional return to the site of her childhood school, almost all of Northwest Minnesota had been home to different bands of Ojibwe Indians. But in 1863, the Red Lake and Pembina bands ceded a huge portion of their land (11,000,000 acres) to the United States Government in a colossal land deal known as the Old Crossing Treaty.[17] Known to possess some of the world's most fertile soil, the most coveted region gained by the government in the treaty was the land in the Red River Valley, the area on both sides of the Red River, which formed the boundary between Minnesota and North Dakota.

During the two decades that followed the cession, the government surveyed and opened the land to homesteaders. They settled first on the fertile Red River Valley land and then, later, on the lands closer to the winding Thief River that would become the future site of County Line School. The government surveyed this area in 1879, and by the end of 1883, the land was nearly all taken.

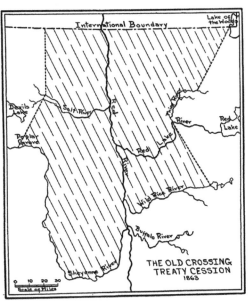

Source: **"The Old Crossing Chippewa Treaty and its Sequel," Minnesota Historical Society, January 8, 1934, 293.**

The Original Settlers

These settlers were mostly immigrants, primarily from Norway and Sweden, with a sprinkling from England and Germany. Looking for a suitable place to start a new life, the early settlers found the location to be nearly ideal. The prairie soil was a deep black loam, superb for farming. There was plenty of timber scattered throughout the area that could be used for constructing houses, barns, and other structures. It could also be used for heating. Certain spots had a lot of rocks that could be harmful to machinery, but many of the immigrants were skilled masons who recognized their value for construction.

They discovered other advantages as well. The long sand ridge on the western edge provided the settlers with a building place that was safe from flooding. There was an abundance of game living throughout the area that could easily be killed for food. And while the winters were cold and snowy, the climate reminded them of their earlier years in Europe and the skiing, skating, and other winter activities that had been such an integral part of their lives.

Once the area was settled, its residents were anxious to provide schooling for their children. The Scandinavians and Germans had a long history of compulsory education and placed a high priority on literacy. Unfortunately, there weren't any public schools available to them.

The First Schools

They didn't have to wait long. Within two years of being fully settled, three school districts were organized in the vicinity. District No. 107 was organized in July 1883 and later became known as the Thief River Falls District (at the time, Polk County).[18] To the north in Marshall County, District No. 17 was organized in November 1883, first known as the Excel District and later as the Steiner District.[19] In the land immediately to the west of the Thief River Falls District, a new district was formed in January 1885, No. 135, later called the City View District.[20]

The first schools in the area were crude. J.H. Hay, Superintendent of Schools in the Thief River Falls District, completed a historical review of his district in 1908. In it, he described the conditions in the first school:

> The first school..., then District 107, was a three-month term in 1883, with Helen Wallin as teacher. A building in the grove near the iron bridge was used, the furniture consisting of a dry goods box for a desk, and planks resting on powder kegs for the seats.[21]

Begun in a small building near the banks of the Red Lake River, District 107 was initially a country school with one teacher and ten students, eight of whom were from the same family.[22] School enrollment gradually increased over the next few years as the unincorporated village of Thief River Falls grew steadily at the confluence of the Thief and Red Lake Rivers.

Furthermore, in 1885 the Minnesota State Legislature passed a compulsory education law that required all of the state's children aged eight to sixteen to regularly attend a public or private school a minimum of twelve weeks a year.[23] School-aged children from the newly settled area of Thief River Falls needed to comply along with the others. Consequently, by 1890, the number of students in District No. 107 was enough to require a second small building and a second teacher.[24]

With a new, large steam sawmill in town and a burgeoning lumber industry in the region, Thief River Falls suddenly turned into a boom town, and the student population began to soar. By 1894, the district had enrolled one hundred and thirty-five students, all housed in a large modern two-story structure named Central School that had been erected the year before.[25]

Central School, Thief River Falls, Minn.

Central School, operating from 1894-1940

Although not as dramatic, the Steiner and City View Districts had also experienced rapid growth, with student enrollment in the 1894-95 school year reaching sixty-three for the Steiner District and forty-six for the City View District.[26] Numbers that high were far too great for one teacher to satisfactorily handle.

Harold Berg, born in 1887, describes the overcrowding and general conditions in the early days of the Steiner School:

> We had three kids in each seat. We had to send half of them outside to play to make room. Shucks, there were over fifty kids. Was no wonder we never learned anything. That was no school.

They only had three books: arithmetic, spelling, and geography. I guess that was the only books we had to begin with. You got to remember, this was over seventy years ago. Was no schools them days. Only had a schoolhouse in Thief River.[27]

With around sixty students in one classroom and only one teacher, one can easily understand why Berg could say there wasn't much learning going on.

The most serious difficulty that many of the earliest students faced, however, was not the crudeness nor the overcrowding of their school buildings, but the long, strenuous walks they made each day to and from their schools. Some of their homes were located as far as three or more miles away, and if a student needed to circle forests and swamps, the distances were even farther. Episodes of severe weather added to the difficulty and made the journeys uncomfortable and sometimes dangerous.

Louis Meyer, another early student at the Steiner School, remembers a frightening experience when, as a very young child, he became lost in a snowstorm while on his way home from school:

> Well, it was snowing pretty hard, and there was no tracks, no road of no kind, just had to walk right through the snow about knee deep. That's when I got turned around. Instead of going north, I landed south. Landed about three, three and one-half miles south from where I should have been. I

landed at the Malberg place. Simonsons lived there at that time, Herman Simonson. His daughter Mabel was going to school at the same time and had been at school that afternoon. When I got there, she was carrying wood into the house from the woodpile in front of the house. She, of course, took me in. My folks and the old Simonsons were neighbors from the homestead days. The next afternoon the Simonsons brought me home. My parents had hunted all of the night before. They looked in all the empty buildings. The storm didn't let up til about noon the next day. Then Hermon Simonson took me home. I guess my parents wouldn't have seen anything of me until the snowbanks were gone the next spring. There were snowbanks right back of the house where we lived that was eight-ten feet high. After I got lost, that was the end of my school days for that term.[28]

More than any other factor, the children's long trips to and from the area's first three schools led parents to petition for a new school during the winter of 1894-95. Overcrowding at Steiner and City View was another contributing factor. As a result, the new "County Line" school in District No. 72-219J was born.[29]

Because the new district was carved out of Districts 107 and 135 of Polk County and District 17 of Marshall County, both county governments granted the petition. Six days after having been granted by the Marshall County Board of Commissioners, a description of the new school district appeared in the January 10,

1895 issue of the *Warren Sheaf*, the official Marshall County newspaper:

> Petition for the formation of a new school district made by Edward E. Engen and others, granted and it was ordered that the following described territory be formed into School District No. to-wit:
>
> S ½ se ¼ and s ½ sw ¼ sec 31 twp 155 rng 43, sw ¼ sec 5 twp 154 rng 43, all sec 6 twp 154 rng 43, all sec 7 twp 154 rng 43, all sec 8 twp 154 rng 43, all sec 17 twp 154 rng 43, all sec 18 twp 154 rng 43, n ½ sec 19 twp 154 rng 43, e ½ and e ½ w ½ sec 1 twp 154 rng 44, e ½ ne ¼ sec 24 twp 154 rng 44, e ½ and e ½ nw ¼ and e ½ sw ¼ sec 12 twp 154 rng 44, e ½ and e ½ nw ¼ and ne ¼ sw ¼ sec 13 twp 154 rng 44, s ½ se ¼ and se ¼ sw ¼ sec 36 twp 155 rng 44.[30]

County Line's district number, 72-219J, was unique, containing two numbers instead of the usual one, and having a J at the end. The 72 in its title was its Marshall County number and indicated it was the seventy-second school district to be organized in that county; the 219 in its title indicated it was the two hundred and nineteenth school district to be organized in Polk County; and the J at the end indicated a joint school district—in this case, crossing county lines.

The Original Territory of School District No. 72-219J

Map Year: 1895

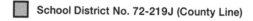

School District No. 72-219J (County Line)

Miles
0   1   2   3

2

The Fred Copp School

Few facts are known about the early years of School District No. 72-219J. If records were kept, they seem to have been lost. Several sources, however, provide morsels of information which, when put together, piece together the likely story.

The Early Years

Alfred Solem, in *Excel Township: A Story of the First Hundred Years*, wrote a brief history of the Fred Copp family: "[Fred] was a schoolmaster and taught Joint District 72-219, known as the County Line School, which at the time he taught, was located on the ridge south of the present Robert Rausch home and a short distance south of the Copp home."[31] This account establishes Fred Copp as the teacher when the schoolhouse was located "on the ridge" but does not specifically tell us for which years. In another article in the book, Solem shares an interesting story that again involves the new school:

> John Engen, on his way to the County Line School, went into the barn of our neighbor to the south, John Kellberg, took his ox harnesses, and hid them in the woods. Years later a close neighbor, Mrs. Fred Copp, found them when she was picking berries. They were now weathered and useless. The

loss of the harnesses was a hardship for Mr. Kellberg, as the early pioneers had very little money to purchase supplies. Mr. Kellberg caught John and gave him a sound thrashing in an attempt to have him confess as to where he had hidden the harnesses. But John was tough and told Mr. Kellberg, "We had a Swede where we came from. We fixed him and we will fix you too."[32]

John Engen lived about one and three-fourth miles north of the Fred Copp home, just off the same ridge. Kellberg also lived on the ridge, his farm adjoining Copp's to the north. In order to reach the Copp farm from the Engen home, one had to cross the Kellberg farm first. If Engen "was on his way to the County Line School" when he stole the harnesses from Kellberg, the schoolhouse was most likely located on the Copp farm at that time.

The 1895 Minnesota Census lists John Engen as a fourteen-year-old son in the the Edward E. Engen family. Because it's unlikely that Engen attended a country school much beyond the age of fourteen, the harness incident probably occurred around 1895, the year the school was organized.

A brief description of the Copp School appears in the 1976 edition of the *Pennington County History*. In a piece written about the family of Lars and Axelina Erickson, the unnamed author describes the primitive conditions of the school they first attended.

There were three children born to them at the homestead. They never had a doctor but had a midwife. Selma Erickson Myrold was born in 1886, Esther Erickson Johnson in 1887, and Frank (Frances) Vernon Erickson in 1900.

Their first school was at the Fred Copp home. They had no desks, so they sat on chairs; they had no paper to write on, so they used slates and white chalk or a slate pencil. Mr. Fred Copp was their teacher. Later they went to school at the North Star School on the sand ridge.[33]

Selma and Esther would have been eight and nine years old in 1895, the year that District No. 72-219J was organized. If the Copp School was their first school, as claimed, the school very likely started on the Copp farm with, as described, Fred Copp as the teacher. There is no mention of a schoolhouse, but it was a common practice in those days to hold classes in someone's home until a schoolhouse could be constructed.

Fred Copp had moved to his home in Excel Township in 1890. He came from the Crookston, Minnesota area

Fred Copp at his home in 1948

where he had also been a school teacher.[34] Because there weren't any schools within three miles of his new farm, it was an ideal spot for starting one. Furthermore, with classes being held on the farm, he didn't need to do any traveling.

Moving the Schoolhouse

The schoolhouse that was built "a short distance south of the Copp home" was moved to a different site. In a piece written by Georgia Muzzy Malberg that also appears in the *Excel Township* book, she describes a "school on the ridge" that was later "moved onto the prairie."

> When the boys were old enough to go to school, they had to attend the Steiner School which was three miles away. Later they attended a school on the ridge, west several miles. This schoolhouse was then moved onto the prairie, which was reached by walking.[35]

A warranty deed found at the Pennington County Courthouse reveals that School District No. 72-219J purchased one and a half acres of land from Frederick Edenholm on March 30, 1903 for thirty dollars.[36] Located in Section 8 of North Township in Red Lake County (changed to Pennington County in 1910), the new site was about three-quarters of a mile east of the Copp place, on the open prairie, and is undoubtedly the same site that Malberg refers to in her article.

No one knows for certain why the schoolhouse was relocated. A likely explanation is that Fred Copp had decided to stop teaching, and the building needed to be removed from his property. By placing the schoolhouse on publicly owned

Change in Schoolhouse Location

Map Year: 1903

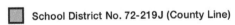

School District No. 72-219J (County Line)

Schoolhouse at Copp Farm Location

Schoolhouse at Permanent Location

Miles
0   1   2   3

property, the district had a lasting home for the schoolhouse and control over its usage.

The School Becomes Known as County Line

Despite its new location, the school continued to be called the Fred Copp School. Gradually, however, its name changed to County Line. It is unclear when the County Line name started being used. It could have been while it was still at the Copp place. Copps lived in Section 7 of the Excel Strip, a mile and a half extension along the south edge of Excel Township. It would have been situated very close to the county line. It could also have started at the prairie site. The one and a half acres of land purchased from Edenholm bordered Marshall County, and the schoolhouse had been placed only a few feet from the county line.

For a period of time, both names were used. A newspaper account in 1912 reported, "The young people of this neighborhood organized a young peoples' progressive society Saturday evening at the County Line Schoolhouse, known as the Fred Copp Schoolhouse."[39]

It's unfortunate that more records weren't kept from those early years. The information we do have, though, is helpful in piecing together the probable story. It appears that the school began in Fred Copp's house with Copp as the teacher in 1895. A schoolhouse was later constructed on the Copp farm, a short distance south of his house. Copp taught the school until 1903, at which time the schoolhouse was moved onto the prairie about three-fourths of a mile to the east. Because the prairie site was school district property, it provided a permanent home for the school. The school, which was originally called the Fred Copp School, gradually became known as County Line.

COUNTY LINE

Neighborhood Quarrel

Across the nation, it was not unusual to have controversy whenever a schoolhouse was moved, or a "breakaway" school district was being proposed. While some affected residents saw their lives benefiting from such a change, inevitably others saw theirs suffering. The most common areas of dispute dealt with travel and financial concerns.

Schoolhouse Move Starts Controversy

Moving the Copp Schoolhouse to the prairie site was especially controversial, and it ignited a neighborhood quarrel that lasted for nearly two years. On April 9, 1903, just nine days after the new site was purchased, several disgruntled neighbors drafted a petition to organize a new school district.[41] That same day, *The Thief River Falls News* reported "The moving of the Copp Schoolhouse has caused so much dissatisfaction that a new school district will probably be formed."[42]

The proposed district would be entirely in Red Lake County and take territory away from three existing school districts: District No. 72-219J (County Line), District No. 2 (first known as the Weberg School, later as the Willowdale School), and District No. 135 (City View). County Line would suffer the greatest impact, losing about one-fourth of its area and fifteen of its thirty-six students.[43]

County Line residents who lived outside of the proposed district were strongly opposed to the petition, feeling their school would be excessively harmed. Nineteen residents sent a letter to the Red Lake County Board of Commissioners explaining their opposition:

Whereas, a petition has been presented to your honorable board asking for the formation of a new school district out of a portion of Joint District No. 219-72, Towns 154 & 155, Ranges 43 & 44 in the counties of Red Lake and Marshall, Minnesota, and other districts of said counties, and

Whereas, said request is believed to be inconsistent with the best educational interests of said joint district and all other territory to be affected thereby, and incompatible with the financial condition of said territories,

Therefore, we, the undersigned legal voters of said Joint District No. 219-72, submit this remonstrance to your honorable body and protest against the granting of said petition.

But after due consideration, if your honorable body sees fit to organize said new district, we ask that Sections 7 & 18 of Town 154, Range 43 be retained unbroken in the old district, namely Joint District No. 219-72 in Red Lake and Marshall Counties.

Signed,

Fred Copp, Emma Copp, C.A. Swanson, L.O. Williams, Fred Edenholm, W.W. Williams, H.R.

Williams, John Kellberg, Andrew J. Rindal, Anton Mortensen, Bernt Johnsen, John J. Baner, John Baner, Jr., Thomas Jacobson, Peter Jacobson, Mrs. Thomas Jacobson, B. Jacobson, Peter Solem, Alvilde Solem.[44]

Red Lake and Marshall Counties Hold Hearings

Because School District 72-219J was a joint district, both affected counties held hearings. At the Red Lake County hearing on July 14th; John Smith, John Finke, and Carsten Christensen argued in favor of the proposal, while Fred Copp argued against. After listening to both sides, the board decided to approve the petition, and they designated the new district as Common School District No. 21.[45] *The Thief River Falls News* reported, both before and after, on the hearing:

> Another important matter to come up before the board at this meeting is a hearing on the petition to carve another school district out of Districts 2, 219, and 135 in Norden and North Townships. Strenuous objection is made on the part of a large number (people) in these districts.[46]

> Fred Copp, John Smith, John L. Finke, and C. Christensen were down to Red Lake Falls the first of the week to appear before the county commissioners and argue for and against the formation of a new school district out of territory in North and Norden. The first named gentleman was

against the new district, while the latter three favored it. The board decided to create the new district.[47]

John Finke had been an important figure during County Line's earliest years. He had been a leader in its formation and had served as one of its first school board members. Upset over the schoolhouse move, he became a leading advocate for a "breakaway district." Prior to the Marshall County hearing held on July 15th, Finke sent the commissioners the following letter:

> Our schoolhouse has been moved more than three-quarters of a mile east and about forty rods north, which makes it almost a mile from its former location. It was moved off from a nice sand ridge and down on the flat prairie where it is now almost surrounded by water, and for those reasons we must form a new district.
>
> The proposed new district does not take in any land in your county, but as it affects Dist. No.72, I'm sending you a copy of the petition. The schoolhouse in the proposed new district will be located three miles southwest from where our old schoolhouse is now.[48]

Despite Finke's letter, the Marshall County Board rejected the petition just one day after Red Lake had approved it. No official explanation for the denial was offered; however, an examination of the petition reveals that it did not have the required signature of Superintendent of Schools Edmund Franklyn.

Yet, the petitioners were persistent. On October 6, 1903, they drafted a second petition with nearly twice as many signatures. The second petition involved the same territory and was basically the same as the first.[49]

Those opposed to a new school district were also persistent. Several contacted the Marshall County Superintendent and again convinced him to not sign the petition. This time Franklyn sent a letter to the Marshall County Auditor, A. B. Nelson, to explain his refusal:

November 14, 1903

Dear Nelson,

Yours received. I cannot sign the petition herewith as it will leave #72 in such condition that it will really put them out of the school business. I have letters from many in this county asking me to refuse the petition. I am sure that it is only a neighborhood quarrel and not a want of school that has caused this petition to be signed. I am,

Yours truly,

E. Franklyn[50]

The Marshall County commissioners held a hearing on November 27th. Minutes of the meeting indicate that the motion to approve was "laid on the table."[51] The petition was revisited on January 7, 1904 when again the motion to approve was "laid on the table."[52] A copy of the petition found at the Marshall County Courthouse, however, clearly shows it was rejected and has the chairman of the board's signature under the rejection notice. As with the first petition, it was never endorsed by the

Marshall County Superintendent of Schools. Apparently, the advocates for the petition were unable to convince Superintendent Franklyn to change his mind.

School District No. 25 (North Star) Formed

Despite the two rejections by the Marshall County Board, a new school district was eventually formed. How it was accomplished, though, is not obvious. A careful reading of the minutes taken at subsequent meetings of both affected counties reveals that no further action on the matter was ever recorded.

It appears that the Red Lake County Board decided to unilaterally move forward on the petition it had approved more than a year before. All of the territory in the proposed school district was in Red Lake County, and the Red Lake County Superintendent of Schools had endorsed the petition. On the form entitled, "Order Forming New School District" that was filled out after the July 14, 1903 Red Lake County hearing, the original district number, 21, has been crossed out and a new number, 25, written above it.[53]

> *be and the same is hereby organized and constituted a school district, and shall be hereafter designated and known as Common School District No.* twenty one *of the County of* Red Lake *State of Minnesota.*

The number was also noticeably changed in the minutes taken during the hearing.[54] Since districts were numbered chronologically and since District No. 26 was approved on May 1, 1905, one can assume the action took place sometime prior to that date.

It is clear from tax records that the new school district began operating during the fall of 1905. Records found at the Red

Lake County Court House show that the county first paid out tax revenue for the 1905-06 school year.[55] The formation of School District No. 25, commonly called North Star, caused County Line to lose a substantial amount of its southwest territory, including all of its land in Norden Township. It also lost several students.

Among the students lost were the children of Carsten and Karen Christensen. The Christensens lived about one and one-half miles south of the Fred Copp farm and on the same ridge. According to a piece written by Helen Christensen that appears in the *Pennington County History*, "The schoolhouse had been built,

School District No. 72-219J Loses Territory

Map Year: 1905

School District No. 72-219J (County Line)

School District No. 25 (North Star)

Lost Territory

but for some reason, had to be moved; so the Christensen home also became a schoolroom for at least two years."[56]

Like the Copps before them, the Christensens held school in their home until a schoolhouse could be built. In 1907 two acres of land were purchased from Ole Rogne in Section 13 of Norden

Township,[57] and the North Star School was erected. School District No. 25 was operational from 1905 to February of 1951.

The loss of land and students did not put County Line "out of the school business" as Superintendent Franklyn had predicted. Fortunately for the district, it never had to go through a similar experience again. During its remaining years, area farmers occasionally transferred portions of their land into or out of the school district, but County Line gained as much land as it lost by these transactions with little impact on its well-being.

Despite a rocky start, the relationship between the County Line and North Star Schools improved. Due to low enrollment, the two schools even held joint classes for the 1926-27 and 1927-28 school years. As the years continued to pass, they shared many special events, and the neighborhood quarrel caused by the schoolhouse move was gradually forgotten.

North Star School, 1905-1951

4

Special Events

The pioneers who started County Line School were family farmers. They were determined to build meaningful and prosperous lives, not only for themselves and their own children, but for their neighbors and their children as well. Farmers had a popular saying at the time, "You are only as good as your neighbor." In a world where their daily lives rarely extended beyond the neighborhood, farmers were keenly aware of their dependence on each other.

Since its founding, the residents of District 72-219J had worked together to make the school an integral part of their neighborhood. Following the move to the prairie location, however, they greatly increased the use of the facility for both school and non-school activities. As a result, the schoolhouse site bustled with activity and quickly became the lifeblood of the community.

In rural areas across the nation, special events were commonly held at country schools. Since every neighborhood had to have a school, it made sense to use the facilities for non-school as well as school events. Schools were in walking distance of their homes, had a building large enough to handle crowds, and were situated on an acre or two of land, making them ideal for outdoor as well as indoor activities.

It was not unusual for others beyond the neighborhood to also attend these events. That was especially true in later years when traveling became easier. Guests were highly valued and, as a rule, were granted special attention. A common method of recognition was to ask the guest(s) to stand and be recognized.

The occasions were often promoted by area newspapers. Small town publishers hired reporters, typically farmwives from the surrounding rural communities, to write weekly columns on the affairs of their neighborhoods. These columns were extremely popular and an effective place to publicize. For many years, the County Line events were covered in the Steiner News and the North News, both of which appeared regularly in the *Thief River Falls Times*. There were a few years in the early nineteen hundreds when the Steiner column also appeared regularly in the *Warren Sheaf*.

Once telephones were introduced to rural communities, it became customary for each neighborhood to have an established "news day" during which its reporter gathered the news by phone. There was a long list of individuals to contact, and the process took up much of a day. It was the responsibility of those organizing the affairs, meanwhile, to get the information to the reporter far enough in advance to get it into the correct paper. They generally wanted to publicize in the issues that came out immediately before and after the occasion.

The County Line School was used for a variety of activities including church services, meetings of different sorts, fall socials (sometimes called carnivals), Christmas programs, contests, graduation ceremonies, and school picnics. Certain occurrences were intended to entertain, while others were meant to worship, inform, honor, or compete. All of the gatherings gave those in attendance an opportunity to socialize.

Each type of activity is discussed in this chapter and then followed by a sampling of newspaper accounts. Two activities are also followed by a reproduction of the program used at one of its events.

Church Services

During the early 1900s, Sunday church services and Sunday School classes were conducted at the schoolhouse. Although information on the gatherings is scant, there are two articles in the *Pennington County History* that provide us with a few useful facts. In a piece on the Peter and Catherine Smith family, the author tells of church services being held at the "Copp School (later called County Line) northwest of Thief River Falls."

> Before any church was organized, services were held in homes by lay preachers and missionaries sent from England by the Methodist Church. Garments, layettes, and other supplies were also sent by groups of women from England. Later, services were held in schoolhouses, one of which was in the Steiner area, and another at the Copp School northwest of Thief River Falls.[58]

In the second article, which covers the history of the United Methodist Church in Thief River Falls, the book again refers to services being held at County Line. The article states, "From 1902 to 1906, Rev. Charles H. Flesher served the church. On alternate Sundays, he preached at the County Line School located three miles north of town."[59]

Although the pastors who preached at County Line were Methodists, the church services were ecumenical. Congregants chose to worship at County Line because it was close to home and filled with friends. Many of those who attended were of other faiths, and some were without any church affiliation.

In addition to the church services, Sunday School classes were also held. In an article on the R. L. Muzzy family that appears in the Excel Township book, the author states, "Sunday School was held in the County Line schoolhouse. Later we became members of the Methodist Church and attended church there, but it seemed as though we preferred to go to Sunday School in the country."[60]

Sunday schools had gained popularity through the nineteenth century. As our nation spread westward, many people of the Christian faith who lived in the East became concerned about the religious instruction of those who settled in the West, especially the young; therefore, a host of missionaries, also known as union organizers, were sent to organize Sunday schools.

In 1912 a union organizer established a Sunday school at the Steiner School,[61] which was located three miles northeast of County Line. For a period of time, both Steiner and County Line had religious schools. Eventually, however, the Sunday School classes, as well as the church services, ended at County Line, and many of the followers went to Steiner.

Joyce Meyer Kron remembers attending afternoon services at the Steiner School as a young girl. Kron, who was born in 1923, explained, "It was convenient for the farmers to have services in the afternoon as it allowed them enough time for completing their morning chores." She added, "When they stopped having services at Steiner, my family started going to church in Thief River Falls. It was sometime during the thirties."[62]

Kron believes that Fred Copp was responsible for starting the County Line church services. Copp was the County Line school teacher at the time and also a staunch Methodist. She believes the services were later moved to the Steiner site because of the differences in road conditions leading to each school. "For much of the year," Kron reasoned, "the road past County Line was impassable with a car. It was a field road. Steiner always had a good road."[63] For a few who lived in the area, the church services they attended at the County Line School, or the neighboring Steiner School, were the only services they ever experienced.

"A new Sunday school was organized last Sunday at the Steiner schoolhouse by the union organizer who has been in this vicinity this spring." ("North of T. R. Falls." *Warren Sheaf*, June 6, 1912, 8.)

"Sunday School was opened at the Steiner schoolhouse last Sunday with a good attendance." ("North of T. R. Falls." *Warren Sheaf*, June 13, 1912, 8.)

"The County Line Sunday School will have a big picnic on July 4th. All are invited, and a fine program is to be rendered." ("Steiner News." *Warren Sheaf*, June 27, 1912, 8.)

"Union Sunday School is being held at the Steiner schoolhouse regularly every Sunday at two o'clock." ("North of T. R. Falls." *Warren Sheaf*, April 24, 1913, 1.)

Meetings

The schoolhouse was occasionally used for meetings, the majority of which were school related. Each summer residents of the school district gathered to have their annual meeting. The purpose of the meetings was to conduct the official business of the district. The Minnesota Department of Education set the dates and provided the agendas to follow. In addition to the annual meetings, school officials periodically called for special meetings as they felt necessary.

There were a few years in which the Progressive Society held meetings at the schoolhouse. Progressive Societies, which were generally known as Farmers' Progressive Clubs in rural areas, were extremely popular in the community from about 1912 to 1918. Rosewood, which was three miles to the northwest, and Steiner also had Progressive Clubs. The clubs were organized by young adults primarily in their teens and twenties.

The aim of the rural Progressive Clubs was to further the cause of agriculture by discussing different methods of farming, new varieties of grains, and so forth. Because the meetings were so popular, it was common for members of one club to group together and either walk, bicycle, or travel by horse and buggy to another club. Progressive Clubs died out rather suddenly after many of the young men left for World War I.

"The young people of this neighborhood organized a young peoples' progressive society

Saturday evening at the County Line schoolhouse, known as the Fred Copp schoolhouse. It started out with a charter membership of about thirty; it is for the purpose of furthering the advancement of agriculture. All farm questions will be discussed. We will try later to give the names of officers, etc." ("North of T.R. Falls News." *Warren Sheaf*, June 6, 1912, 8.)

Fall Socials / Carnivals

Each year the County Line School hosted a fall social that also served as a fundraiser. The proceeds were used for covering the costs of the annual Christmas program and certain school needs. Because all of the country schools in the area hosted similar events, the dates were carefully arranged among the teachers to give everyone an opportunity to attend as many as possible.

The main attraction was an auction in which the boys bid for the right to share a meal with an "unknown" girl. The girls each brought a lunch in a basket or box to share with the highest bidder. What was bid on, however, varied from event to event. Rebecca Halvorson Solem described some of the variations in an article she wrote on the nearby Riverside School.

The young people very much enjoyed them and liked to be able to attend them all. There were basket socials, when the young girls decorated boxes filled with delicious lunches; rag ball socials, when the girls put their name inside of a big rag ball; shadow socials, when the girl's shadow was displayed on a curtain; hand socials, when the girls showed their hands above a curtain; broken heart socials, when part of a paper heart was sold and had to be fitted to the part retained by the girl; and several others. Auctioneers were appointed and the bidding was usually lively, especially when a certain fellow was determined to be the high bidder on a certain basket or whatever. When the sale ended, the fellows found their partners and enjoyed the lunches brought by the girls. Others in attendance were able to buy bag lunches.[64]

Solem went to school at Riverside as a child and later had three sons who were students at County Line. She attended several of the County Line socials.

What took place following the auctions changed over the years. During the teens and twenties, the crowds entertained themselves with singing games like "Farmer in the Dell" and "Skip to My Lou." According to Emily Jacobson Johnson, who was a County Line student from 1918 to 1925, "After the baskets were sold and the lunches had been eaten, the desks would be pushed to the sides and round singing games would be played."[65]

Singing games were eventually replaced by an assortment of fundraising games. The affairs became known as carnivals. There were games for people of all ages. Young children liked playing fishing pond, ring toss, and pin the tail on the donkey. Older children and adults preferred bingo. The teachers supervised as the older students took turns running the games.

A small fee was charged for playing each game, and a fair amount of money was usually raised.

Raffles were frequently held in conjunction with the socials. Tickets for a valued prize were sold prior to and during the affairs. The winning ticket was always drawn near the end of the events. The prize was frequently a homemade quilt made specifically for the occasion by a woman in the community.

> A basket social will be held in the County Line schoolhouse Friday, December 1. Before the social, a program will be rendered by the school children. Arnie Solem will open by a welcome address, after which many fine recitations, songs, and dialogues will be rendered. ("Steiner News." *Warren Sheaf*, November 29, 1916, 4.)

> A dust cap social was held at the County Line schoolhouse Saturday evening, Nov. 22. The party was well attended. About 34 or 35 dollars is reported to have been taken in. Parties present report a good time and parted long after midnight. ("Steiner News." *Warren Sheaf*, December 3, 1919, 8.)

> The balloon social held at the County Line School last Wednesday evening was very well attended in spite of the bad roads and snowbanks. A neat sum of money was taken in to be spent for Christmas. ("Steiner News." *Thief River Falls Times*, December 3, 1931, 10.)

> Margaret Hanson, who teaches the County Line School near Dakota Junction, will have a basket

social at the schoolhouse next Friday evening October 20th. ("Rosewood News." *Thief River Falls Times*, October 19, 1933, 4.)

Let's all go to a necktie social at the County Line School, 3 ½ miles north on highway, 1 mile west, and ½ mile north on Friday evening, October 25th. Ladies, please bring lunch for two and a necktie. Everyone welcome! Elizabeth Jorde, teacher. ("Public Notices." *Thief River Falls Times*, October 21, 1935, 7.)

Bernice Halvorson entertained on Sunday the cast who took part in the play at the County Line social, namely Alva and Alvin Grytdal and Margaret and Jerold Rude. After the dinner, the bunch were treated to a show at the Falls Theater. ("Steiner News." *Thief River Falls Times*, October 30, 1941, 10.)

Christmas Programs

For most residents of the County Line School District, the Christmas programs (often called "A Christmas Tree" at rural schools) were the highlight of the school year. Because the expectations were great, so was the pressure on the teachers to properly organize the events. The lines needed to be memorized, costumes had to be prepared, and hours and hours of rehearsal were necessary in order to make the productions as perfect as possible.

Everyone in the community showed up for the festivities. As they entered the room from the back, they saw a large evergreen tree standing near the front with real candles. It was on the side opposite the potbelly stove and had lots of carefully wrapped presents underneath it. Rows of desks and benches (planks resting on empty nail kegs) had been placed on either side of the room, and there was an aisle down the middle. A single gas mantle lantern, hanging from the wall, gave light to the room.

The crowds took their seats and suddenly became quiet as the programs were about to begin. Two students opened the curtains (white bed sheets draped over wires) from the middle as the acts were introduced. There were readings, recitals, skits, plays, and Christmas carols. Occasionally, an act was interrupted by darkness when a shortage of oxygen caused the lantern to burn out. It would quickly be pumped for air and relit while someone else opened the door to let in the fresh winter air.

During certain programs, Nativity plays were acted out as someone read the second chapter of Luke from the Bible. The plays recreated the scene of Jesus' birth and explained how Jesus and his parents, Mary and Joseph, were visited by shepherds and wise men. It was a tradition to close the programs by having everyone sing "Silent Night."

When the programs were over, gifts for the children were exchanged by drawing names. That was followed by passing out bags filled with candy, apples, and nuts to everyone. Occasionally, Santa Claus stopped by to greet the children and hand out the gifts and treats. They were truly festive occasions.

County Line School Christmas Program
December 19, 1941

Bernice Halvorson - Teacher

1. Song.............................. "Joy to the World"............................... School
2. Welcome ....Doris Rausch and James Arras
3. "Why We Keep Christmas" .... 5 Children
4. Recitation ...."Flight of Christmas" ....Dorothy Muzzy
5. "Aunt Sarah's Tooth"... Dialogue
6. Recitation.............................. "A Letter" .... Arlen Solem
7. Recitation....................... "A Christmas Wish" .... Marlene Kellberg
8. Song............................. "Bells of Christmas"..................... Lower Grades
9. Recitation..................... "Christmas Partnership"..................... Lowell Rude
10. Monologue .... "Message of the Chimes" .... Curtis Swanson
11. "Strange Gifts" .... Dialogue
12. Song........................... "Oh Come All Ye Faithful"............... Upper Grades
13. Recitation ...."To Remember at Christmas"......... Senora Swanson
14. "Christmas at Sand Flats".. Dialogue
15. Recitation......................... "Bobby's Query" .... James Muzzy
16. Song............................. "Away in the Manger" ....Muriel Copp
17. Song.................................... "Silent Night" ....School,
audience join in on last stanza
18. Recitation ...."In Closing" .... Doris Rausch

"There was a Christmas tree and program in the County Line schoolhouse Thursday evening. Miss Esther Kellberg, the teacher, was the leader. It was not very well attended on account of bad weather." ("Steiner News." *Warren Sheaf*, December 27, 1916, 8.)

"The school children of County Line School had their Xmas tree and program in the schoolhouse Friday night. A fine crowd was present and a good time reported." ("Steiner News." *Warren Sheaf*, December 24, 1919, 9.)

"On Wednesday evening this week, Miss Margaret Hanson, a local girl who teaches the County Line School near Dakota Junction, will have a program and Christmas tree, and a number of local folks plan to attend." ("Rosewood News." *Thief River Falls Times*, December 24, 1931, 4.)

"A number of schools had their Christmas tree and programs Friday night. Steiner, Riverside, and Groven School and on Saturday night, the County Line School." ("Steiner News." *Thief River Falls Times*, December 24, 1942, 7.)

Contests

Throughout its history, County Line participated in a variety of contests with other country schools; however, it was especially true during the twenties and thirties. Among the competitions that were popular at that time were spelling bees, declamatory contests, and play day athletic events.

Spelling bees and declamatory contests often required an elimination contest prior to the events because the number of participants from each school was limited, usually to four. That was not the case with play day, when everyone could participate. Winners of the different contests advanced to a higher level of competition.

The first levels of competition were sectional events in which County Line students competed against students from two or three neighboring schools. Since County Line competed mainly against schools from Marshall County, its winners, along with the winners from the other schools, normally advanced to a countywide competition held in Warren, the county seat and largest city in Marshall County.

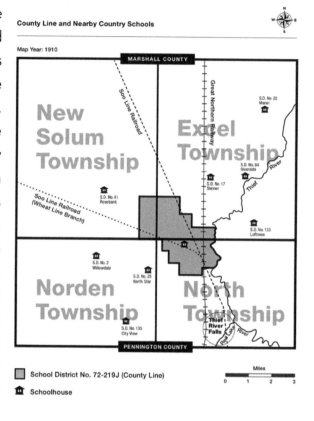

County Line and Nearby Country Schools

Map Year: 1910

School District No. 72-219J (County Line)

Schoolhouse

Because of poor accommodations, County Line rarely, if ever, was chosen to host a sectional contest. Besides having an inadequate road, it had other disadvantages as well. For indoor activities, the main problem was its size. Measuring only eighteen by twenty-six feet, the schoolhouse was one of the smallest in the area. For outdoor activities, the schoolyard wasn't acceptable either. There were low areas where the ground was always spongy and when it rained, would frequently be filled with water.

The spelling bees took place in early February. Typically, there were three or four students from each school. The crowds were not large. They consisted mainly of parents, grandparents, and a few other interested people. Unbiased judges were carefully chosen ahead of time to lead the contests. The contestants stood in a line and took turns as the judges announced the words for them to spell correctly. As each competitor misspelled, the individual had to sit down. The winner was the last contestant standing.

Spelling bees had sectional, county, and regional levels of competition. The regional event was called the Red River Valley Spelling Contest. It was held at the Crookston Winter Shows late in February and attracted large crowds. The size of the crowds often frightened contestants and caused many of them to prematurely misspell.

The declamatory contests were held late in the school year. Participants were divided into two classes according to grade. Those who were in grades three through five competed in Class A. Those who were in grades six through eight competed in Class B. Each school could have two contestants in each class. The winners from each class moved on to countywide competition. If they were fortunate enough to win there, they advanced to statewide competition held at the Minnesota State Fair in St. Paul.

Contestants in declamatory contests were required to deliver a speech by memory in front of three judges. The speech had to be completed in a given amount of time, usually around three to five minutes. The judges, meanwhile, evaluated the competitors by their delivery, voice, use of gestures, and other criteria. Declamatory contests were popular and attracted big crowds.

Play day contests were also held near the end of the school year. Occasionally, schools scheduled play day in conjunction with the declamatory sectionals. Play day contests consisted mainly of track and field events including races of different lengths, running broad jump, and high jump. Separated by gender, slightly different events were held for each. For example, girls ran a fifty yard dash, whereas boys ran a sixty yard dash.

Other types of athletic events that were held included potato races for the girls and pull ups for the boys. Winners of the different categories advanced to countywide competition that took place at the park in Warren. It was held on the same day as the rural school graduation ceremonies, which were later in the day.

"Play day was held by the river two miles east of here on Friday. Five schools participated in the numerous contests. Starting in the morning, they all enjoyed an open air dinner and ended the day by playing bat ball." ("Steiner News." *Thief River Falls Times*, May 18, 1933, 16.)

"The sectional play day was held at the Skomedal Park Friday. Five schools competed, and an agreeable crowd took advantage of the fine weather. The bat ball game was won by the Steiner School with County Line winning second place and Loftness third. Racing, high jumping, balancing, and chinning were some of the contests the enthusiastic youngsters took part in. Raymond Rupprecht of Sunny Side School receives special mention in his excellent feat of chinning sixteen times, making a record far above any others." ("Steiner News." *Thief River Falls Times*, May 10, 1934, 7.)

"The sectional play day was held at the Sordahle School Friday, May 3rd, with six schools participating. The winners are as follows: Verla Merkins, Ollie Nelson, Luyda Ose, LeRoy Rodahl, Perry Grytdahl, and Joe Rausch. The team winning the bat ball was the Manor team." ("Steiner News." *Thief River Falls Times*, May 9, 1935, 10.)

"The sectional declamatory contest, with four schools taking part, was held at Riverside School on Friday night. Lewis Meyer of Steiner School received first prize and James Copp of County Line School won second prize in Group A. The winners in Group B were Mildred Jensen of County Line School, first prize and second prize went to Anne Hillyer and Alice Austinson (tie). The judges were Mrs. Reap and Mrs. Korstad of Thief River. Lewis Meyer and Mildred Jensen will take part in the declamatory contest at Warren on May 16th. Our heartiest congratulations go to the winners." ("Steiner News." *Thief River Falls Times*, May 21, 1936, 11.)

"Winners of the Minnesota Quiz contest from County Line School are James Muzzy, Senora Swanson, and Marie Nelson. The contest was conducted at the Willowdale School." ("Steiner News." *Thief River Falls Times,* April 20, 1944, 16.)

Graduation Ceremonies

Graduation ceremonies occurred at the completion of each school year. In order to receive their diplomas and be promoted to high school; however, students first needed to pass the state board examinations. Because the results of the tests were so important, teachers spent weeks in advance preparing the students.

A day was set aside for test taking. Both the seventh and eighth grade students needed to participate. The seventh grade took the geography exam. The eighth grade took the arithmetic, science, history, and English exams. As soon as the tests were completed, they were sent to the state to be corrected. Generally, everyone passed.

During the school's early years, the graduation ceremonies took place at the schoolhouse. At the time, it was a custom for each of the graduates to contribute to the program by sharing a talent they had developed, such as delivering a recitation or reading an essay they had written. School officials, and occasionally one of the county superintendents, handed out the diplomas.

From the early twenties and on, the ceremonies changed. During that period, County Line graduates joined with graduates of the other rural schools to have countywide ceremonies. Since County Line was a joint school district, depending on which county they lived in, certain graduates went to Warren for the ceremonies and others went to Thief River Falls.

County Line School Graduation Program

May 12, 1911

Teacher – Clara Backe

Graduates: Ruth Esther Kellberg
Alice Catharine Solem
Lida Josephine Muzzy

1. Music
2. Essay ------------------ "Both Sides of Woman's Suffrage" ---------- Alice Solem
3. Music
4. Chalk Talks -- Little Girls
5. Music
6. Recitation ----------------- "The Ride of Jennie McNeal" -------- Esther Kellberg
7. Music
8. Essay -----------------------------"Evangeline" ----------------------- Lida Muzzy
9. Music, Recitations, etc. --School
10. Address---Mr. J. Hay, Superintendent, S.D. No. 18 (Thief River Falls)

Class Colors – Red and White
Class Flower – Red Carnation
Class Motto – "Push Forward"

"The following pupils from County Line School went over to North Star School to take the examination: Arnie Solem, Julius Liden, Vernon Copp, and Miss Goldie Kellberg." ("Steiner News." *Warren Sheaf*, March 28, 1917, 3.)

"Last Wednesday was a red letter day in the history of the rural schools of the county. Three great educational events had been scheduled by David Johnson, County Superintendent of Schools,

53

to take place on that day; namely, the County Play Day, a School Officer's Convention, and the eighth grade graduation of 112 pupils from the rural schools of the county. These events brought to the city a large number of boys and girls from different parts of the county, their parents, teachers and friends, and also some 150 district school officers. Many of the children from the distant parts of the county had the pleasure of visiting Warren for the first time and considered it quite a treat.

The program began at 10 A.M. at the high school auditorium with the enrollment of school officers, followed by an excellent address on 'School Finance' by Hon. J.M. McConnell, State Commissioner of Education. Afterwards until noon, a number of the county play day contests were pulled off at the ball park.

After the noon intermission, the play day contestants, rural school graduates, and school officers formed in parade line and headed by the Warren Juvenile Band marched several hundred strong through the principal streets of the city, making an interesting sight.

After the parade, some more play day contests took place at the ball park. Roy E. Luttrell, Assistant County Superintendent of Schools, directed the various contests in the presence of a large number of spectators. The winners in the various stunts are published elsewhere in this issue.

The school officers assembled at the high school building at three o'clock with Supt. David Johnson presiding. George A. Selke, Rural School Inspector, gave an excellent address followed by a general discussion of school questions from the school board's point of view.

The graduation exercises were held at the high school auditorium in the evening, when 112 pupils who have finished the eighth-grade work of the rural schools were granted diplomas. The boys and girls were seated on the stage and presented a fine appearance. Marshall County and The State of Minnesota surely have reason to be proud of this splendid lot of young people who had come from homes in widely scattered parts of the county to receive a certificate for work finished and well done.

The exercises began with an invocation followed by an address of welcome by Supt. G. Holmquist of the Warren schools. Supt. Johnson presented the class to the State Rural School Inspector, who in turn in a happy speech presented the class to the State Commissioner of Education, Hon. J. M. McConnell. Mr. McConnell, after having heartily congratulated the boys and girls upon their good work in finishing the prescribed course of study for the rural schools, gave an educational address that was replete with wise thought relative to schools and the training of young people. Time and space forbids a more extended mention. He was pleased, he said, to be in Marshall County and to note the interest and progress made in the rural school work. He complimented County Superintendent Johnson upon his energy, ability, and efficiency in directing and supervising the rural schools of the county. He also said that he approved of the play day contests, holding that the development and strengthening of the children's bodies by play was an important part of their education, a part that has hitherto been much neglected.

After Mr. McConnell's address followed the presentation of the diplomas to the graduates by County Superintendent Johnson. 'America' sung by the audience closed the very interesting exercises." ("Big Day for County Rural Schools." *Warren Sheaf*, June 21, 1922, 1.)

School Picnics

It was a tradition to end the school year with a picnic. The details of the picnics varied considerably from year to year. Occasionally they were held at the school, but

Photo above: Carol Jaennette, Roger Solem, Muriel Copp, Stuart Solem, and Philip Jaennette raking dead grass

frequently they were not. It was more common to hold them at scenic locations such as along the banks of the Thief River to the east or among the oak trees on the sand ridge to the west. For a few years, they were held at parks in Thief River Falls.

Often the entire neighborhood was invited. These were pot luck affairs in which each family brought food to share. When not eating, a variety of activities were available for all age groups. Most of the older men played horseshoes, whereas softball was more popular with the young crowd. Perhaps more importantly, the occasions provided a perfect opportunity for everyone to socialize.

When the picnics were held at the school, it was common to start the day by cleaning the school grounds. Some of the students formed lines and raked the yard while others cleared the flax straw banking away from the schoolhouse. The waste was then hauled away and burned. The day culminated with a picnic, often by building a bonfire and roasting wieners and marshmallows.

Stuart Solem and Spencer Johnston pulling wagon loaded with grass

Sometimes the students' families joined them for the roast. These occasions were also known as cleanup day.

"Miss Esther Kellberg gave a party last Monday afternoon for her school pupils and their families, at the home of her parents, Mr. and Mrs. John Kellberg. A large crowd was present and all report a merry time. Members of the following families were present: Best, Copp, Christiansen, Jacobson, Muzzy, Myer, Liden, Solem, Williams, and Miss Hattie Lundgren." ("Steiner News." *Warren Sheaf,* June 6, 1917, 2.)

"County Line children and teacher, Miss Halvorson, met at the school Thursday to get their reports and put away their books and to top it all off, they had nectar, ice cream, and cake." ("North News." *Thief River Falls Times,* June 5, 1941, 16.)

"Miss Bernice Halvorson, who has taught in the County Line School for two years, closed her school Friday, and a picnic was held at the schoolhouse on Sunday. Miss Halvorson will spend a week at her parental home, after which she will leave for Bemidji to attend teachers training. Miss Halvorson will also be teaching her third term in the County Line School this coming year." ("Steiner News." *Thief River Falls Times,* June 4, 1942, 5.)

"The County Line School closed on Friday, and the pupils and parents enjoyed a picnic dinner at the Tourist Park in Thief River Falls on Sunday. Miss Joyce Meyer has returned to her home at Steiner. She will again teach the County Line School next year." ("Steiner and Agder News." *Thief River Falls Times,* May 30, 1945, 10.)

Other Events

Over the years, County Line students took part in many other events as well. On certain holidays such as Halloween, Thanksgiving, Valentine's Day, and Easter, parties were generally held at the end of the school day. The students' families came, a short program was rendered, treats were served, and games were played by the children.

On other holidays such as Arbor Day and Armistice Day, the occasions were observed, but in a more solemn, respectful manner. On these days, the daily routine was set aside, and the time was spent teaching virtues such as patriotism and good citizenship. Guest speakers were often invited to assist.

Some events randomly took place. They included such occurrences as open houses, birthday parties, farewell parties, nature hikes, and tours. These types of events were handled differently from teacher to teacher.

"Miss Esther Kellberg, who teaches school in the County Line schoolhouse, gave a Halloween picnic for her scholars last Tuesday. All reported an enjoyable time." ("Steiner News." *Warren Sheaf*, November 8, 1916, 7.)

"Arbor Day was observed in the County Line School Friday afternoon." ("Steiner News." *Warren Sheaf*, May 9, 1917, 2.)

"The school nurse will be at the County Line School Thursday, Oct. 10 in the morning and would like for the mothers to be there if possible. The pupils in County Line School and their teacher, Miss Halvorson, went on a nature hike Friday. There are 16 pupils in our school, with 12 having perfect attendance." ("North News." *Thief River Falls Times*, October 3, 1940, 3.)

"County Line pupils and teacher, Miss Halvorson, had a nice valentine party Friday which was enjoyed by all. Ice cream, cookies, and cocoa were served, and valentines were given out." ("North News." *Thief River Falls Times*, February 20, 1941, 8.)

"The pupils in County Line School and teacher, Bernice Halvorson, went on a tour Friday. They visited the Times, City Dairy, and Jung's Bakery. They had dinner in the park which they all enjoyed." ("North News." *Thief River Falls Times*, October 2, 1941, 14.)

"A large crowd attended an open house Friday evening at County Line School." ("North News." Thief River Falls Times, November 12, 1942, 4.)

"The County Line pupils and Miss Meyer had a little party on Friday in honor of Janice and Donna Rood, who expect to leave soon." ("North News." *Thief River Falls Times*, April 4, 1946, 10.)

"County Line pupils and teacher Clara Mae Jorde entertained the mothers with a program and a lovely lunch for Halloween Friday. There was also a cake in honor of Arlen Solem's birthday; Spencer Johnston, who left to make his home in Middle River; and Warren Kron, who moved to Thief River Falls." ("North News." *Thief River Falls Times*, November 6, 1947, 10.)

Conclusion

Involvement in special events was a valuable part of the students' school experience. It enhanced their personal growth by developing skills, building self-confidence, and teaching them the value of working together.

The occasions also helped build a close-knit community by providing everyone with an opportunity to socialize and have fun. Life in rural areas was often lonely, and their residents needed the companionship the gatherings offered. As for the students of County Line, it is what they remembered best and held dearest about their school years.

5

Remembrances

All of the former students of County Line who could be found were asked to contribute to this chapter in one of two ways. They could either write an essay or be interviewed on their memories of attending the school. In response both methods were chosen. The lone surviving teacher was also asked, and she chose to be interviewed.

During the process of locating former students, it was discovered that only around fifteen ex-students were still alive; and of the fifteen, nearly half had attended the school for three years or less. Consequently, a few children of deceased students were also asked to contribute. Three more offerings were gained as a result.

The chapter is divided into eleven segments, each of which focuses on a former student or teacher. Each segment begins with the person's memories of the school and ends with a brief summary of his/her post County Line life.

Senora Swanson Almquist
Student: 1938-1947

Senora's Memories of County Line School
as Submitted in Writing

County Line School was located on the line between Marshall County, to the north, and Pennington County, to the south. The Wheat Line Branch of the Soo Line Railroad was situated a short distance south of the school site, and there was a raised ridge less than a mile away to the west. Three trees stood on the west side of the schoolhouse, and a lilac bush grew near its southeast corner.

Besides the schoolhouse, the only other building was a

Senora Swanson

wood/coal shed with outdoor toilets, boys and girls, on the north and south sides. We did not have "store bought" toilet paper. Rather, we used a catalog, newspapers, or during fruit season, the wrappers from peaches and pears.

There was a road running along the west edge of the schoolyard. This was the only road leading to the school. It was not a maintained road. So in the winter, it was passable only with horse and sleigh.

Coal was hauled in by horse and wagon to the coal shed. Wood was cut and split and stored there as well. Edwin Swanson,

Steve Jaennette, and Alfred Solem would help with the coal and wood. Edwin would cut wood at Uncle Charlie's homestead. Ray Rausch and Vernon Copp often helped. Edwin would leave early in the morning with horse and sleigh. The men would wear big heavy coats and large fur mittens; good for holding onto the reins of the horse. They would, at best, keep your hands from freezing. Long woolen underwear with woolen pants and four-buckle overshoes helped to keep the cold at bay. Scarves, wrapped around the face, and earlaps, pulled down on the caps, helped to insulate whatever remained exposed to the winter winds. The wood was cut into large chunks and then was split. The men used large saws and axes. Since it was cold, most of the wood split easily. However, there was always the stubborn chunk with knots! The small pieces were used as kindling to light the fire. The larger pieces burned in the potbelly stove to warm the room and the students.

The stove was quite large and round in the middle, thus its name "potbelly." It sat in the northeast corner of the schoolhouse. The teacher was responsible for making the morning fire. Often there were coals from the day before. This was to make sure that the school was warm and welcoming for the students walking or skiing to school. In addition to heating, the stove served as a source for cooking. Each child would bring his or her noon lunch from home. We carried our lunches in dinner pails. In the winter, the students would heat up their lunches on, or close to, the big stove. We often brought soup or hotdish for lunch.

There was no running water at the school. Each child carried his or her own water. Often it was carried in a small tin pail (honey pail) with a lid and handle. In the winter, the water would freeze on the way to school. The big potbelly stove would thaw the ice so we could have drinking water.

Bringing water to school was not the only use for the water pails. In the spring and fall, striped gophers would dig holes in the school yard. After school, or during the last recess, the students would pool all of their water into one pail and then pour it into the gopher hole. The wet gopher would pop up out of its tunnel and run all over the yard, chased by the school children. Sometimes the gopher would drown in its tunnel. At other times, the children would catch the gopher and kill it. If it was attempted during recess, which the teacher did not approve of, the children did not have enough time to catch the gopher and only lost their water. In those days, children could turn in gopher tails to the county agent for money.

County Line School was not equipped with electricity. There was no air conditioning and no electrical lighting for evening meetings or programs. In fact, there was not even a yard light. So when special evening activities occurred, such as the Christmas program, people would sometimes bring their own lanterns to light the room.

The Christmas program was a major production. Our family, like many others, would arrive at the evening Christmas programs in a sleigh drawn by horses. We lived two miles from County Line School. It was a cold ride at 30 degrees below zero. Our sleigh had sides on it. We would huddle under heavy blankets, wrapped up as best we could to stay warm. The horses would be waiting outside the school when it was time to go home.

Everyone was excited about the program. We had new homemade dresses for outfits. There were no slacks for the girls in those days. Girls wore heavy, long underwear and brown stockings. We struggled to hide the lumps of underwear, trying to look our best. The boys usually had shirts with ties. There were no knit pullover tops. Home knit sweaters were very common. Home knit scarves and mittens were common Christmas gifts from our parents and were always welcome in the cold winter.

I remember one particular incident when a severe winter blizzard set in while we were at school. This blizzard started very quickly and was severe and dangerous. Letting school out early was not an option since the children would have to walk or ski home, potentially becoming caught in the blizzard. The stove had run out of wood, and the schoolhouse was getting cold. It was considered too dangerous for anyone to search for the woodshed in the storm. My father, Edwin Swanson, started out for County Line School to rescue the students who lived in our direction from the school. He stopped and picked up Chris Jensen on the way. They arrived at County Line School and loaded up the sleigh with children. We were wrapped up in heavy blankets. There was no top on the sleigh so the winds howled and the snow blew over and around us. On board were my brother Curtis, Roy Rude's boys, Duane Jensen, and me. When we got to Jensen's, the visibility was zero. My dad feared for our lives since he could not see anything in front of him. He told us that we might not make it home, so we began to pray. Dad let go of the reins and let the horses find their way home. They took off in a gallop and brought us safely home. They knew instinctively the way home, road or no road, even in a blinding storm. Their nostrils were completely iced over, but they still found the breath necessary to do their job.

Walking was the usual mode of transportation to County Line School. In the nice days of spring and fall, it was a delight to see the children walking to school from the north, south, and west. There was a walking path along the fence line leading west. Both families of Copps walked down that path. From the north came the Muzzy, Jeannette, Solem, Kellberg, and Rausch children. From the south came the Swanson, Jensen, Rude, and Rood children. Donna Rood went to County Line School for only a short time. Curtis and I sometimes walked the Soo Line Railroad tracks to school, along with the Jensen and Rude children. This shortened the distance. At times, when I would walk the rail tracks alone, a trolley car carrying a working rail crew would stop and pick me up and give me a ride to school. When that happened, the trip was quite fast. As you think of modern dangers, no one would dare let a girl ride the rails with rail workers. All the children were safe walking alone or in groups. It was so different from today.

The Swanson home was located by the Dakota Junction of the railroad. Trains frequently went by, especially during the fall when the grain was being shipped. Sometimes "bums," unemployed men traveling the rails in search of work, would hide in the box cars. When the train switched at the Dakota Junction, they would jump from the cars and run across the field. Sometimes they would hide in our barn hayloft. Many times they would come to our house and ask for food. Mother would give them a sandwich and a cookie in a brown sack and then ask them to leave. This commonly occurred.

In the winter, I would ski across the countryside on homemade skis. My father made them by forming a point on a narrow board. Then he would soak the point in water to make it bend upwards. The bend was made by hooking the tips to rafters in the barn and letting them dry. As the winter wore on, the bends would flatten. This made skiing more difficult, so the bending process would be done again.

At County Line School, there were children in grades one through eight. In a way, this was an advantage. The lower grades would watch and listen to the instruction being presented to the upper grades. This gave the fast learners in the lower grades a head start on the next grade. The slow learners received a review of the lesson the next year. Being a fast learner, the teacher would often ask me to help the lower grade students understand the problem or question. Today, schools hire teacher aides to help with such tasks.

We had many chalkboards throughout the room on which assignments and questions for a particular class were written. During each class, the teacher would use the blackboard to demonstrate arithmetic problems, list spelling words, and so on. We did not have an abundance of paper, so the blackboard served many purposes.

Many of the students had specific jobs assigned to them. Each job assignment would last a week. For example, some students would clean the chalk erasers by pounding them together outside of the schoolhouse. This would release great clouds of chalk dust. Other students would wash the blackboards at the end of the day. We had to have the coal bucket filled with coal from the shed. Wood was needed to be carried in and put in the wood box. This included both kindling and the larger chunks. Wood was used to get the fire hot before the coal could be put into the stove. Another assignment was to keep the overshoes in straight lines under the coats that hung on hooks. Students were assigned to keep the library books in order, not sticking out or crooked. Another student was assigned to ring the hand bell when school started and when recess was over. Many of these jobs could be completed in five minutes or less before school let out.

We had a recess in the morning and one in the afternoon. At noon we ate our lunch fast so that we had more time to play before school resumed. We did not have any playground equipment. We did not have swings, slides, teeter-totters, or even balls and bats. Whatever balls and bats we used came from our homes. During recess we played games such as bat and ball (softball), pump pump pull away, last couple out, hide and seek, tag, drop the hanky, and here we go around the mulberry bush. When spring arrived, we would sail a stick in the ditch and watch it go through the culvert. Did we sometimes get too close to the water when retrieving the stick for another sail? Oh, yes! When a student misbehaved, the punishment was losing their recess. That was, by far, the worst punishment. Recess was such a fun time that discipline was not much of a problem.

During the winter, we would have snowball fights. Forts would be built out of snow chunks. There was competition between the boys and girls to make and throw snowballs. Once in a while, a girl would get permission to be on the boys' team. This happened only because a certain boy liked her.

All of the grades at County Line School studied reading, arithmetic, history, geography, spelling, science, language, and writing (penmanship). We practiced making letters both in print and cursive. A great deal of emphasis was placed on penmanship. Page after page we practiced making letters. Doing our best was always encouraged. We did not have a lot of homework. We were given time to do homework when the other grades were receiving instruction. Test times were often an opportunity to bring home a book. Spelling words were written on a piece of paper, tucked in our pockets or dinner pails, to take home and practice. Proper spelling was also considered very important.

We used flash cards to drill addition, subtraction, multiplication, and division. Older students would often flash the cards for younger students during rain or storm recess. If we were quiet, the teacher sometimes let us practice in the corner of the room while she was having class. Competition was a great way to learn them quickly.

In addition to arithmetic and the other core subjects, we had an art class. This was a class in which we designed and built crafts. Before Christmas, we constructed gifts from wood to give to our parents. May baskets were another big project. We would get whole sheets of pretty colored construction paper and make May baskets. Then we would fill them with nuts or raisins. Candy was a little too expensive and, therefore, a treat that children could not afford. Sometimes we would include a wrapped peppermint candy. After making the basket, we would identify some special person or home and leave the basket at the door. We would take off running so that we would not be seen, and the gift would be anonymous. Of course, this happened on the first day of May.

We also made valentine boxes for the exchange of valentines. These boxes were made at home from shoe boxes or oatmeal cartons. They were brought to school the day of the party. Many of the valentines were also homemade. There was a contest to see who could make the prettiest valentine box. The best valentines always were given to the teacher. Often the mother of one of the students would send cookies for the Valentine's Day party.

County Line School began each day with the students standing, facing the flag, placing their right hand over their heart, and reciting the Pledge of Allegiance. We often sang the national anthem, "The Star-Spangled Banner." The fifteen minutes, or so, before noon was music time. We would sing songs such as "Old Black Joe" and "Massa's in de Cold, Cold Ground," just to name a couple. We did not have a piano, so the starting note was given with a pitch pipe, a round instrument with all the notes of the scale. Starting in October, we sang Christmas carols in preparation for the Christmas pageant.

We had large maps of the world that the teacher would pull down in front of the room. These helped us locate a place or country we were discussing in history or geography. The round globe was used in geography, as well as in science, to demonstrate how the earth rotates on its axis. In addition, during fall and spring, we would take nature hikes during which we identified grains, wild flowers, and any animals that we saw.

County Line School did not have any means of emergency medical treatment or evacuation. We had a box of Band-Aids in the teacher's desk drawer. We did not have any blankets or pillows in case someone became ill or if the stove failed during the winter.

Despite what now appears to have been hardship, County Line School provided a wonderful education to all of the children because we genuinely cared for and loved each other. Families made a strong commitment to the school, to education, to each other, and to our country.

Post County Line

Following high school, Senora attended teacher's training in Thief River Falls. Afterwards, she taught for two years at a country school located a few miles north of Oklee, Minnesota. Like most country schools, it was a one room building with no plumbing or electricity. To get to work each day from her rural boarding home, Senora walked two miles carrying food, water, and an arm full of school books.

Senora married Basil Almquist in 1953. During the first few years of their marriage, they lived and farmed near St. Hilaire, Minnesota, which was Basil's hometown. While living there, they began a family of four, three boys and a girl.

The family moved to Lucan, Minnesota in 1957. Six years later, they moved to Cummings, North Dakota. At both locations, Senora started home-based businesses that are still active today. In Lucan Senora started a business of doing seamstress work. The business specializes in designing and sewing wedding gowns and attendant gowns, but it often takes on other sewing jobs as well. After moving to Cummings, Senora added cake baking and decorating as a second business. Senora and Basil are presently living in Cummings.

Marlene Kellberg Anderson
Student: 1943-1946

Marlene's Memories of County Line School
as Submitted in Writing

I really don't recall a lot about County Line since I attended school there for only first and second grade. My dad sold our farm shortly after I started third grade. My sister Dalys went to County Line for part of her first grade. We then moved to Thief River Falls and attended school there.

I have good memories of living on the farm. Joyce Meyers, who taught at County Line School, lived with our family at the time. It was fun to have her there. She even allowed me to occasionally help correct papers, but I wonder how much help I really was. I was told that my mother taught there at one time also. It must have been before I was born.

I would guess that it was about a mile to get to County Line School, which was located straight east from our farm. That made it pretty handy, especially in nice weather. When it was cold, my dad would sometimes go ahead to get the heat going so it would be warm for us. We usually walked, but when it was cold and snowy, my dad would give us a ride in a sleigh pulled by our horses. I think some neighbors would hook a ride with us then also. At other

Marlene (left) and Dalys Kellberg

times, neighbors would meet us at our house, and we would walk together. Dad made me some skis, but I guess that was a bit much for me to handle, because I don't remember using them. They were heavy, and I was pretty little. I also remember playing softball during recess. The reason that stands out in my thoughts is because someone threw the baseball bat and it hit my sister in the chest. She fell down and was knocked out for a short time. When she came around, she was fine. I don't know what they did to help her, but I was really scared. It is interesting how that incident is still so vivid in my mind.

It's too bad that all children can't have the experience of living on a farm and going to a country school. I think it gave us a strong foundation and a hands-on education. For example, I got to watch calves being born. My job was picking the eggs from the henhouse with my grandpa. I also helped Dad clean the barn. During the spring and summer, Mom and I brought lunch to the men in the field. That is when they taught me how to shock the wheat. My sister preferred staying in the house, but I was always outside.

Post County Line

Marlene currently resides in Fargo, North Dakota, where she has lived for most of her adult life. Her husband Gary, who was also from Thief River Falls, passed away several years ago. Marlene was employed as an assistant to the Director of the Fargo YMCA for twenty-eight years. It was a job that she immensely enjoyed.

Dorothy Muzzy Blodgett
Student: 1938-48

Dorothy's Memories of County Line School as Shared by March 5, 2015 Interview

(Q) Can you describe the inside of the schoolhouse?

"We entered the room from a small entryway on the south end. There was a piano in the back by the

Dorothy Muzzy

clothes hangers. The clothes hangers were on the back wall, and the piano was in the southwest corner along the sidewall. The only times it was played while I was there was during recess when the kids fooled around with it.

There was a blackboard on each sidewall and two more in the front. The teacher put the assignments for the students on the sideboards. The students in the lower grades had their assignments on one side, and the students in the upper grades had their assignments on the other side. The boards in front were used to work on lessons during class. If she had new words for us to work with or problems to work on, we used the front boards.

There was a telephone on the west sidewall towards the front, about in line with the teacher's desk. It was a great big one. Only the teacher could use it.

On the other side of the teacher's desk was a large stove that was used for heating. It was located in the northeast corner. There was another stove, a small, two burner gas stove in the back. You lit it with a match. It was real small, smaller than the standard stove. You could use it for heating water to wash dishes. Sometimes, when it was real cold, we would light it in the morning to get a little heat in the back. It was near the door on the east side.

The library was fairly big. It was in the back of the room on the opposite side from where the clothes were hanging. The books came from the Thief River Falls Library. We could keep them for so long and then they needed to go back. Then we got a new bunch."

(Q) Did the wood stove adequately heat the building, and who cared for it?

"It was a cold schoolhouse, I'll have to say that. The floor was so cold that I would sit at my desk with my feet off of the floor for much of the time. To stay somewhat comfortable, I kept shifting their position, sometimes placing one foot on top of the other. If it got too bad, she (the teacher) would let us come up and sit around the stove.

The outhouses were attached to the woodshed. When the older kids went to the bathroom, they had to carry an armful of wood back in with them. We burned some coal but mainly wood. The teacher would put coal in the stove before she left for the day. That was her job. The coals lasted longer than wood and the school wouldn't be as cold in the morning. If the teacher wasn't there for some reason and the kids were looking after the place, they were always supposed to use the wood, not the coal."

(Q) Who were some of your teachers, and what do you remember about them?

"Bernice Halvorson was one teacher. She stayed with the Solems and was teaching at County Line when Arlen (Solem) started school. They would walk together, but when they got to the County Line road, Arlen liked to stay behind and play. James and I were living in Marshall County at the time. We had to walk along that same road. We were told that when you see Arlen, to bring him along to school.

I remember we got invited to Miss Halvorson's wedding. She had such a pretty outdoor wedding. I thought that it was a dream wedding. It was at the Halvorson farm.

They had a wreath decorated with flowers and they walked through that. I don't think that she was our teacher at the time, but I had been her student. That was probably the first wedding that I can remember. To me, it was like a fairy tale. It was so pretty, and then for her to invite us was really special because we weren't relatives. When a lot of other people got married, it was just the relatives that were invited.

Joyce Meyer was another teacher. I remember that she would go out and play with us during recess. It wasn't just recess when she joined us either. If we carried wood, she would carry wood. We felt close to her because she associated with us. She played ball and other games with us and didn't stay inside. She was always right there with us.

The last teacher I had at County Line was Clara Mae Jorde. Because I was related to Clara Mae, it was expected that I help her. When you're one of the older kids, you can stay an extra ten minutes and help sweep the floor or do some other chore. She didn't ask me for help. I think it was my folks who felt I should help so that she could get home a little earlier."

(Q) *You had three siblings who also attended County Line School. Do you have any special school related memories involving them?*

"I never traveled to school by myself. That is because James was older than me, and before he finished, along came Philip. When I went with James, sometimes we skied to school and sometimes we rode our bikes. When I went to school with Philip and Carol, the only time that I could ride a bike was when they were sick or, for some reason, not going to school. If they walked, I had to walk with them. That was because of their age.

We followed the roads and sometimes cut through the fields. It depended on what the weather was like. We found out that sometimes it was easier to walk on the railroad tracks. They didn't clear all of the roads during the winter. I don't think that the last half mile (before County Line School) was ever plowed.

Carol and Philip Jaennette, fall of 1948

When it was cold, we wore snow pants. If it was really cold, I would wear jeans that James had outgrown, but I had to have a dress too. If you had jeans underneath, you were supposed to take them off when you got to school. We also had coats and scarves to wrap around our heads and faces. On our feet, we wore lined boots that were kept on all day. We had homemade mittens on our hands. Sometimes we had two or three pairs on at once.

I don't know why, but James didn't always go to school at County Line. When James was in the first grade, he would go across the river and walk to school with the Jordes. He would cross the river by Lida and Ray's (Muzzy). I'm not sure what the name of the school was. He would walk with some of Carl Jorde's kids.

My sister Carol broke her arm during recess at County Line School. It was winter, and she was on her way to the bathroom. There was a drift of snow in front of the outhouse. She slipped and fell onto the ice. We were living on the Marshall County place at the time. Carol stayed at home until her arm healed, and I brought her homework to her from school. She was probably in first or second grade."

(Q) *What do you remember most about your school years?*

"The large neighborhood gatherings. In the fall, County Line would have a carnival. Everyone would get together. There was a raffle where the kids would sell tickets for a blanket or something like that. There was always a place to play bingo. One had to pay a little bit, and if you won, you could pick out a prize. They also had a fishing pond. They had some curtains that were hung in a circle. We really tried to decorate the school well.

Then there was a Christmas program in December, before the break. They always had a bag of treats. Santa Claus would come and hand them out to everyone. It might have been Alfred (Solem) sometimes. I don't know who it was. We drew names and then exchanged gifts. Depending on who the teacher was, sometimes we got gifts from them also. The tree was always pretty big. The kids would decorate it with paper chains and things we made in school. Muriel Copp could sing and she usually sang a solo. We also sang together as a group. At the end of the program, everyone sang "Silent Night."

In the spring, we had picnics. A lot of the times, it would be held at the Solem place up on the ridge.

Everybody in the community would come, not just the kids. We had ballgames and horseshoes and other contests. Usually, the men would play with the kids, and the ladies would be in the house fixing lunch. Everybody brought something to eat."

(Q) *After you graduated from County Line, you attended Lincoln High School in Thief River Falls. How did the schools compare?*

"County Line and Lincoln were very different. In Lincoln, you had a modern bathroom and running water, and you had a locker where you could keep your clothes and other items. My days at County Line were also a good time. I enjoyed it. It seemed that we worked well together as a unit, and all of the kids were equal."

(Q) *You attended County Line at the time James Rude was badly burned and eventually died. Can you share your memories on James and that terrible tragedy?*

"James was in the same grade as me, and we were both looking forward to going to high school. We were going to be big people then! I remember us talking about that on the day we took our finals. We had to take tests to pass grade school before we could go on to high school. They were called the state boards. The only ones who had to go to school that day were the ones who were taking the test. It was for those in the seventh and eighth grades. Muriel Copp was one year behind us, so she probably was there with us.

I do remember when he got burned. It wasn't very long after we took the finals. They were going to have the school picnic at his place. He was cleaning up an area for the picnic. He was burning some of the trash when he caught on fire. I knew that it was serious, but I didn't think that it would be terminal."

Post County Line

Following high school, Dorothy married Ned Blodgett, a career Air Force soldier. His occupation required them to frequently move, and they lived in various cities around the U.S. and abroad. During this time, Dorothy worked intermittently as a licensed practical nurse. She was also kept busy raising their three daughters.

After Ned's retirement from the military in 1976, the family moved to Thief River Falls. Ned entered the teaching profession and taught at different schools in the area until his sudden death in 2005. Dorothy remains living at the family home.

Muriel Copp
Student: 1941-1949

Muriel's Memories of County Line School
as Submitted in Writing

County Line School provided excellent individualized instruction. Later in my life as a technical college instructor, individualized instruction became the big "new" buzzword, but this is how I learned at County Line School. For most of my first eight years of school, I was the only one in my grade and moved along at the pace in which I learned best. Looking back, I have an even greater appreciation than I did at the time for those young teachers who had only a couple of years of preparation to teach. They had to do a lot of learning on the job, as well as managing all of the courses for eight different grades. In so many ways, I believe my education was better than, or as good as, my contemporaries in the city schools who

Muriel Copp

had many children and one teacher for just their grade level. By the time I was in eighth grade, there were only about eight children in school, so not all grades were needed.

Much was gained from listening to the other classes in their scheduled times of instruction. There is one word I will never misspell (maybe others too, but this one is very specific!) because a younger class was learning that "There is 'a rat' in the word separate." How very many times I saw that word misspelled on student papers when I was teaching! In a one room school, it was pretty much impossible to tune out the other classes no matter how quietly they were being conducted in another part of the room. Then, too, there were always other things to do when my lessons were completed. Sometimes it was helping the teacher with things like rubbing sheets of blank paper on a tray of gel to obtain purple copies similar to what the fluid duplicators produced in a mechanized fashion. At other times, it might be working on an art or craft project or picking up a book to read.

Possibly the only areas in which I might have received better preparation for high school were physical education (which

I disliked!) and music (which I loved!). We certainly played games, but there weren't enough children to have teams and positions such as I was expected to know when I hit physical education classes as a high school freshman. Our rules were somewhat sketchy, but sportsmanship was always enforced. Music was often singing a patriotic song after the Pledge of Allegiance to begin the school day. There was a small pump organ in the school, but it was hardly ever played, and I don't remember it being used during singing time.

As indicated earlier, County Line was a true one room school, a square, small building sitting on the prairie with few trees or bushes around it. The only other building on the property was a woodshed with a toilet at each end of it, one for the girls and one for the boys. The children carried their own supply of water to school - mine was in a little glass jug on a rope to make it easy to carry. There was a pump, but the water was undrinkable.

There was no electricity, so several kerosene lamps were attached to the walls on brackets. They were seldom lit unless there was an evening activity in the building or the day was very cloudy and dark. The windows were tall and let in good light.

There was no basement under the school and no furnace. In the fall, tar paper was nailed up outside at the base of the wall and straw banking was packed against it to help keep out some of the winter cold. There was a big jacket stove in the front corner of the room, and the teacher had to come to school early to start the fire. On the coldest days of winter, the first classes were held huddled around the stove. One particularly severe winter, we had school around the big dining room table at the Rondorf home for a few days.

REMEMBRANCES

From time to time, there would be little parties at the end of the school day with treats, such as before Halloween, Thanksgiving, and Valentine's Day. I particularly recall a Valentine's Day when mother had made strawberry Jell-O with bananas in it (my favorite) in a glass casserole (no Tupperware!), and tied it up in a towel for me to carry to school on my skis. There was a snowbank right outside the entryway to the school where I fell and broke the casserole. I'm sure the teacher had to mop up a lot of tears along with the Jell-O!

In the fall, there was usually one evening when families came to the school. There were games for the children. One was called "fishing pond," where older children would pin a prize on a rope attached to a pole thrown over a curtain. I don't recall if there was a program or if food was served (I'm sure there was a plentiful supply of goodies!). The event was probably intended for the parents to become better acquainted with each other, the teacher, and the children other than their own. Sometimes Bingo would be played for a few prizes, which were rounded up by the children and the teacher.

There was always a Christmas program put on by the students for their parents and other family members. The teachers were apparently expected to prepare this event, much like a Sunday School program (which wouldn't be allowed today!). Children were given recitations to memorize, sometimes there were little plays or skits, and always there was group singing. Since I loved to sing, I was usually given an opportunity to do a solo or sing with a small group of children.

The final event of the school year was usually a picnic. We often spent a day raking the school yard and then had a bonfire to toast marshmallows or roast wieners. When the gathering was with the families, I believe it was a potluck. Usually there would be a softball game in which parents participated too.

A sad note on the end-of-year picnic occurred when I was in the seventh grade. The Rude family had offered their yard for the picnic the year their youngest son, James, completed eighth grade. On the Saturday before the planned event, the rest of the family had gone to town, but James stayed home, wanting to clean up the yard, especially for the picnic. He started a fire and threw some gasoline on to get it going. Unfortunately, the gasoline flashed, and he caught on fire. He rolled on the ground to put out the fire and went to the neighbors for help. After a long time at Children's Hospital in St. Paul, he died from his injuries.

Most of us walked to school until the snow came. Then we used cross country skis, which were nothing more than boards with points on one end and a strap in the middle to slip your foot into. Some of us had book sacks to carry extra belongings, such as lunch, water, and extra scarves or mittens. By my last couple of years in country school, a few children had bicycles. The road to the school was gravel and sometimes nearly impassable. When walking or skiing wasn't good (especially in the spring), I would walk to school on the railroad track, which went right past our farm. A special treat was a ride with the section line men who happened by on their "speeder."

All of us carried lunch, and in winter most of us carried something in a small glass jar that could be heated up. The kerosene stove would be started, and a pan of snow put on to melt. When it was melted, the lunches in glass jars would be placed in the pan of water to warm until lunchtime. Jobs were assigned, so we took turns getting the pan of water ready and loosening jar lids to allow for any expansion of the food while heating (favorites were usually macaroni hot dishes or soup). Some water would also be heated for washing hands. In warmer months, hand washing would be done outside. In the winter, however, it would be done over a big enamel pan. One child would be assigned to pour the water, another to apply homemade soap, and yet another would hand out the paper towels for wiping hands.

Other assigned tasks for recess time included sweeping the outdoor toilets and making sure there was paper available and carrying in wood for the stove or, in later years, a scuttle of coal.

There was always some game to be played, usually softball, in the fall and spring. Other favorite games were dodgeball, ante-I-over the woodshed, pump pump pull away, tag, and captain may I. In the spring when a sheet of ice formed on the playground or an adjoining field, we would get some branches and a piece of coal and play our version of hockey. Once in a while, the boys would like to pour water down a gopher hole to see if they could get the poor drenched little animal to come out. We were creative in entertainment because there were few pieces of equipment – a softball and bat, a basketball but no hoop, a football to practice throwing, and occasionally something brought from home.

Post County Line

Muriel graduated from Bemidji State Teacher's College in 1957 with a degree in Business Education. She began her career in education by teaching at the secondary level, including three years at the high school in Red Wing, Minnesota. While there she accepted a postsecondary teaching position at the Red Wing Area Vocational Technical Institute where she started the school's Secretarial Clerical Program. She remained at the school until her retirement in the spring of 1993. Later in life, Muriel married Sam Pearson, and the couple are currently enjoying their retirement years living in Red Wing.

Shirley Nelson Jasperson
Student: 1946-1948

Shirley's Memories of County Line School as Shared by September 21, 2014 Interview

(Q) What do you remember about County Line?

"I don't have many memories of the school because our family moved from the area during my third grade. I remember having basket socials when the girls would prepare baskets and the boys would buy them on auction. There was an older boy who bought mine. I didn't want to eat with him and I didn't.

One time I walked home from school with Arlen Solem. Arlen knew where there was a cigar that his dad had from someone's birthday. We went upstairs in the garage and smoked it. We got real sick! It was funny that we didn't burn the building down.

I also remember having Clara Mae (Jorde) as a teacher. Curtis (Swanson) would sometimes drive her to school in the mornings and pick her up afterwards. That was before they got married. That's about all I remember."

Post County Line

In 1954 Shirley married Thorman Dahle, a Korean War veteran. They had two children, Sherryl and Micheal. For a short period during the late 50s, Shirley and Thorman owned and

Shirley Nelson and Arlen Solem

operated a store in Rosewood, Minnesota. Thorman's primary job, however, was serving as a mechanic at the Tunberg Motor Company in Thief River Falls. Thorman died in 1985.

Shirley later married Russell Jasperson, a farmer from Plummer, Minnesota. They too had many good years together. Both of them liked old-time music, and they often listened and sometimes danced the waltz to it.

Shirley preferred working and being busy. During her life, she held several different jobs. Perhaps most noteworthy was a long-lasting job at Digi-Key Corporation in Thief River Falls, where she worked a total of twenty-two years. Shirley also had several hobbies. Among her hobbies were embroidery, quilting, crocheting, sewing, cooking, and gardening. Furthermore, she enjoyed doing jigsaw and crossword puzzles and was known by her friends for being a great hostess. Shirley died in 2015 from heart related issues.

Emily Jacobson Johnson
Student: 1918-1925

Among the children of deceased students who contributed to this chapter was Lee Johnson, son of Emily Jacobson Johnson. Lee knew about this project and, when contacted, was eager to help. A day or two after being contacted, he brought some family pictures that could be used for the project along with the book *Pioneer Tales: A History of Pennington County*. Found in the book was an account of his mother's childhood memories of being raised in Pennington County. What follows is the portion she wrote concerning County Line School.

Emily Jacobson at home

Emily's Memories of County Line School as Taken from
Pioneer Tales: A History of Pennington County

"Mabel Kellberg was my first teacher. She had beautiful red hair. We used to open school by singing songs from an old brown book that had lots of Steven Foster songs; Civil War songs like 'Tenting Tonight,' 'Battle Hymn of the Republic,' 'Just the Battle Mother,' and also the same Christmas carols that we now sing. After noon recess, she began class by reading a chapter from a book. I remember the first book was *Anne of Green Gables.* In my mind, Mabel Kellberg was Anne Shirley of that book, red hair and all.

Desks were all double at that time. At first we would have to sit two at a desk. It was awful hard to not whisper once in a while to such a close neighbor. In later years, there were enough desks so everyone sat alone. There was a fine new teacher's desk in front. In the rear, there was a big bookcase for library books that must have been eight feet tall. In front, behind the teacher's desk, was a tall cupboard where all the textbooks and school supplies were kept. No one was allowed to open the door except the teacher. In the back of the room, there were hooks for the pupils to hang up their wraps. A table was there for them to put their lunch buckets on. These were mostly syrup pails with a hole or two punched in the lid to let in some air. The children also had to bring water from home in pails.

Before school, at recess, and at noon, there would be lively games of hide and go seek, tag, pump pump pull away, sheep in the pen, and many others. In the spring, someone would bring a cloth ball that was made by wrapping strips of cloth around a small pebble. A covering of denim or other strong cloth would be sewed on the outside. Ante-I-over would be played over the schoolhouse and games of one o' cat played with a homemade bat.

Two big events during the year were the fall social and the Christmas program. The social was held to raise money to buy Christmas candies and apples to be given out at the Christmas program. Vivian Copp was always the auctioneer at our school.

Most of the time, the baskets sold from fifty cents to one dollar and twenty-five cents. But once in a while, a couple of young blades would vie to see who could get what they thought was the teacher's basket. It was usually the prettiest one. One time they did this and got fooled. One of the women had outdone the teacher.

After the baskets were sold and the lunches had been eaten, the desks would be pushed to the sides and round singing games would be played. I can still hear Filmore Malberg leading the singing of such games as 'Farmer in the Dell,' 'A Brand New Pig in the Parlor,' 'Captain Jenks Came Home Last Night,' 'There is Somebody Waiting,' 'Four in the Boat and the Boat Goes Around,' 'Four Old Maids in the Skating Rink,' 'The Needles Eye,' and 'Happy is the Miller that Lives by the Sea.' These were all round games played by joining hands into a circle, with one or more persons inside the ring choosing partners as the song indicated. Once in a while, a change would be 'Skip-Come-a-Lou' to vary the game. Dancing was never allowed at County Line School. At Steiner School, dancing was permitted, and they used to get much bigger crowds at their socials. A lot of young people from town came after the baskets were sold and the lunch was eaten. There were other games that were played outside during the day like drop the handkerchief, late for supper, and last couple out. In all of the games and amusements, very little equipment was needed. That which was needed was either something on hand or something that could be made with little or no expense.

The Christmas program was the highlight of the year. There always was a big evergreen tree with real candles. Gifts were exchanged after the program had been given. Bags of candy, apples, and nuts were given to the children. Otto Saugen was always asked to light the candles, and everyone kept a sharp eye on them to see that the tree didn't catch on fire. Then the kids would be bundled up and put into the sleighs for the ride home. By the time they reached home, the little ones would be sleeping and needed to be carried into the house by their mom or dad. The older ones hurried inside to warm up by the fire and to look at the gifts that they had received."[66]

Post County Line

After graduating from high school in 1929, Emily went back to school and took a year of teacher's training. She taught at an area country school for one year and then decided to leave the profession.

In 1931 Emily married Lloyd Johnson, a farmer from St. Hilaire. During the early years of the marriage, Emily worked alongside Lloyd on the farm. When their three children were old enough to care for themselves, however, she took a position at the JC Penney store in Thief River Falls. It was a job that she diligently worked at for many years. In 1976 Lloyd died from a heart attack, and Emily died about a year later from cancer.

Rudy Rude
Student: 1939-1942

Rudy's Memories of County Line School
as Shared by his son Joel in an April 21, 2017 Interview

(Q) Did your father ever share stories with you?

"Yes. My father once told me a story involving himself and his younger brother James. One day at school, James was sitting outside on a wooden bench eating his lunch when some older boys came over to bully him. One of the boys lifted the far end of the bench causing James to fall onto the ground and spill his lunch. Dad saw what happened and began fighting with the boys. When he went home from school that afternoon, my grandfather

All five of the Rude children went to the County Line School
Left to right: Jerold, Rudy holding James, Lowell, and Margaret

could see that Dad had been in a fight and wanted to know what had happened. After hearing the explanation, Grandfather said, 'If it happens again, take off your belt to use as a whip and make sure the belt's buckle is at the end that strikes.' Dad followed the advice, and the bullying ended."

Post County Line

Rudy began working for Clifford Hedeen Construction of Thief River Falls when he was only sixteen years old. After a few years, he left in order to start his own business of dozing and hauling gravel. Because the work was seasonal, Rudy took on a variety of side jobs during the winter months, including one as a Thief River Falls police officer.

He was married to Helen Henrickson of Goodridge on January 1, 1956. The couple had four children, two boys and two girls. The family lived on Rudy's boyhood farm, which was located a short distance southeast of the County Line School.

Rudy was a person who relished life. When not working, he liked to socialize with friends and relatives. He was musical and often played his accordion during the get-togethers.

Rudy passed away in 2009. His two sons, Joel and Jim, now run the business he once started.

Alfred Solem
Student: 1913-21

Alfred was interviewed by the author and a mutual friend in January of 1987, several years before his death. At the time, the intent of the interview was to gather some personal stories on Alfred's life. Among the many stories he told, a few were about County Line School.

Alfred's Memories of County Line School
as Shared by January 6, 1987 Interview
with Peter Solem and Loiell Dyrud

(Q) *Did you like school?*

"I never liked school. Sometimes I even put flour on my face to look pale when I didn't want to go. Of course they could see that. One time Dad said to Mom loud enough that I could hear from upstairs, 'Guess we better call Doc Melby to see what's wrong with Alfred.' Then I got ok! I wanted to be

Alfred and Arnie Solem in their new suits

home…around the barn. In the summertime, I wanted to be outdoors. Everybody has his place. School was no place for me."

(Q) *Were there any Christmas programs at County Line School that were memorable to you?*

"There is one that I remember. We were supposed to go down to the Christmas program at the school. We had to speak our piece. Dad had walked to town to buy suits for my brother Arnie and me. We were waiting for him to get back, and it was almost time to go. He finally came with the suits. My brother got his first one with long pants, and I got one with mittens. Then we all walked to the school."

(Q) *Can you recall any other stories about County Line?*

"There is another story. It was a little bit before my time. I might have been born, but it was my brother Otto and my sister Alice that told me about it. There were two Roesnors. They called one Coffee and the other one Bawlah. The one always had a bottle of coffee along for lunch, and the other one bawled all the time. Coffee and Bawlah. Bawlah had a poem for Christmas. He was real scared and didn't want to get up in front of the crowd. Then after a long awkward pause, he suddenly dashed to the front, turned to the crowd, and raced through the poem *Little Jenny Wren* so fast that no one present could understand a word. (Alfred then mimicked Roesnor by racing through the poem in a similar manner. After a few moments, he repeated the poem at a slightly slower than normal pace.)"

COUNTY LINE

A little Jenny wren,
Was sitting by the shed.
She wagged her tail,
And nodded with her head.

She wagged with her tail,
And nodded with her head.
As little Jenny wren,
Was sitting by the shed.

"He said it real fast because he wanted to get it over with. Then he ran back to his seat and sat down. That was Bawlah Roesner."

Alfred Solem (closest to teacher) getting exercise during recess with other students

Post County Line

Like a lot of farm boys from his era, Alfred ended his formal education after the eighth grade in order to focus his efforts on farming. When his father's health no longer permitted him to do farm work, Alfred took over its management. In 1935 he married a neighbor girl, Rebecca Halvorson, and together they had six children.

Being gifted with handling livestock, Alfred raised a variety of farm animals. He is perhaps best known for developing a high-quality herd of registered Black Angus cattle. In 1980 Alfred turned the ownership of the farm over to his youngest child, Peter, but he continued to work on the farm until the summer of 1993, at which time his failing health necessitated a move to a local nursing home. Alfred died in 1995 at the age of eighty-nine.

Roger Solem
Student: 1943-1949

Roger's Memories of County Line School as Shared by September 3, 2014 Interview

(Q) *Were there any trips to school that are especially memorable to you?*

"Vernie and Alma (Johnston) lived south of us on the ridge, where Knotts live now. They had two children who went to County Line, Spencer and Barbara. We would go by their place on the way to school. One morning Vernie drove us

Roger Solem

(Solem and Johnston children) to school in his Model A. There were a couple of mud holes on the dirt road that were too deep for the car. Vernie drove off the dirt road and went across the field to the east instead. When he came to a drainage ditch running east and west, he gunned the engine and we flew across. We made it to school ok. The Johnston house burned down in the late forties, and they moved to the Greenbush area."

(Q) What do you remember about cleanup day at the school?"

Gary Mason lived where Curt and Carol (Johnson) once lived, north on Highway 32. He would bring his family's Model A truck to school for cleanup day in the spring. We would take the flax straw from around the schoolhouse, haul it away, and burn it."

Roger (right) and Gary Mason cleaning the flax straw "banking" in the spring

Post County Line

After graduating from high school in 1955, Roger served in the U.S. Army for two years, including a one year stint in South

Korea. He then returned to the Thief River Falls area where he worked as a separation machine assembler at a local manufacturing plant for more than forty years. During much of this period, he also raised registered Angus cattle on his farm. Roger is currently enjoying retirement by spending quality time with his family and caring for a small collection of farm animals.

Stuart Solem
Student: 1945-1948

Stuart's Memories of County Line School as Shared by November 9, 2014 Interview

Stuart Solem

(Q) You lived quite a distance from County Line. Can you describe what your journeys to and from the school were like?

"I went my first four years to County Line. Traveling to school wasn't as convenient as it is now because we didn't have any buses to make it to country schools. When we went to County Line, it was about two miles by road. Shirley Nelson and Jimmy and Marilyn Mattson, who lived west of the ridge, would walk up to our place. We would gather and walk south to the corner. There we would meet up with Dalys and Marlene Kellberg, and later on, with Spencer and Barbara Johnston. So sometimes there was quite a crew walking together to school. We just kept picking up people as we went.

Later on, some of the older ones had bicycles and the younger ones didn't. My dad told my mother that he thought they needed to buy me a bicycle because I was walking, and the older ones had bikes. Dad got me a bicycle that was real small. He bought a girls' bicycle because I couldn't reach the pedals on a boys' bike.

Seated L to R: Clara Mae Jorde (teacher), Muriel Copp, Carol Jaennette, Shirley Nelson. On bicycles L to R: Dorothy Muzzy, Stuart Solem, James Rude, Roger Solem, Marilyn Mattson, James Mattson, Philip Jaennette, Arlen Solem

As we got more adept with the bicycles, some of us would show off. We would play a type of 'chicken' where we would ride our bikes towards each other and try to 'tick' handlebars. It was kind of dangerous. Our parents never knew about it. We did that east of the ridge.

On the way home from school, some of the neighbors would cut across the fields. Others would take the road, even if it was a little further, so that we could be together longer. So coming back from school was a little different than going. Those who lived south on the ridge, like the Copps and the Kellbergs, would cut across the fields to go to school. But coming home, they frequently followed the roads with us up to the ridge, then turned back south to go home.

We didn't always go right home either. Sometimes, we would cut across the field with Muriel (Copp). We knew that her mother, Elsie, would have cookies on hand. She always had cookies. I also remember going over to Gary Masons. He lived on the Muzzy place. He liked to box, so he put boxing gloves on us, and we would do a little boxing. All of us Solem kids went over there quite a few times. I think we went over there during the summer vacation too.

In the wintertime, we would ski to school. I learned to ski about the time I learned to walk. My dad bought me a pair of six-foot hickory skis with quite a bit of bend to them. They were nice skis. Arlen, Roger, and I would ski across the fields to school. Mother would first wrap us up so that we could just peek out of our scarves. Arlen would make the path. Roger would be right behind Arlen, and I would be right behind Roger. The three of us would ski across the fields. Our skis had just a strap to hold the foot in place. The snow would sometimes ice up under our heel and cause the ski to fall off. Part of the trip was through woods. I remember how nice it was where we could go through the woods. Our paths would stay clean, and we could stay out of the wind. It did get windy skiing across the fields."

(Q) *What kind of clothing did you wear to school?*

"In the winter, we wore long underwear under our coveralls. Coats would go over the coveralls and then mom would wrap our faces and heads. It was cold, but we really didn't think much about it. It was just the way it was.

We wore hand-me-downs and I was the third down. Arlen would wear a shirt. Then Roger would wear it. Then I would wear it. My mother made clothes out of feed bags because they had designs on them. Arlen was a little chunkier than we were when he was young. He had one shirt that had little pigs on it. I used to tease him about that and he would chase me. He couldn't catch me, though.

As far as shoes, we would sit on top of the table and my mother would draw around our feet to determine the size. Then they would order shoes out of Sears & Roebuck Catalog. That's the way they used to size feet. By drawing around them on a piece of paper and sending it in. Each of us boys had one pair of shoes. We would wear them to school. In the summertime, we usually went without shoes. But we did wear shoes to school even when it was nice weather. My mother would scrape the manure off of them and make sure they were clean.

I told my brother Roger not too long ago that we must have smelled a little bit in school. Roger said that we were clean and that everybody was the same way. That's the way it was in those days. We weren't the only ones who smelled, but we never thought about it either. That was never an issue with us. I look back and think about some of those things now, but I never did at the time."

(Q) *How were the class periods organized?*

"All of our desks faced the teacher. At the front of the room, the teacher had her desk right in the middle facing us. She would sit there looking back at the students. She would set a few desks out in front of her. Then she would call out classes by saying something like, 'Third grade math.' The third graders would all go up there and sit in those desks. There were eight grades of school but there weren't students for all eight grades. Most of the time, there probably were only four or five grades out of the eight."

(Q) *Are there certain special events that stand out for you?*

"Christmas programs were huge in country school. It was something that everybody participated in. We would practice and have rehearsals. All the parents would come for the program. We would have it no matter what the weather was like. One time we had Clifford Jorde come over with his plow when we had a great big storm. The wind was blowing, the snow was flying, and we had big banks that would fill in right away. At that time, there was no road, really, with ditches. Clifford went back and forth clearing out a road. He left snowbanks in the fields on both sides.

We (the Solem brothers) sang 'We Three Kings' at County Line. Adeline (Everson) was the teacher that year.

Arlen, Roger, and I stood up in front. I can still remember. Arlen was on the east side. Roger was in the middle. I was on the west side. We faced the class and sang 'We Three Kings of Orient Are.' We were all dressed up like kings, as good as we could do.

We had an old crank-up phonograph that mom would bring for the programs. The case would open up. Then you would crank it up on one side, and an arm would come down from the other side. Everyone would sing along to the Christmas songs. Some students would get up and do readings. It was a pretty good program that we did. It was a big thing.

I also remember getting together on work day when we had to rake the yard. People would line up and go across the yard with rakes. I think it was on the last day of school. We'd clean everything up. Then we had play day. It was also towards the end of school. We would go to other schools. We went up to a school by Carpenters one time. I remember Randy Carpenter and I were on the high jump and we were down to just the two of us. He beat me, but I felt pretty good because I had never high jumped before. It was probably three feet. I know it wasn't very high."

(Q) *What do you remember most about your years at County Line?*

"What I remember most about school at County Line was going to school, coming home from school, Christmas programs, play days, and flashcards. Adeline would put up addition, subtraction, multiplication, and division flashcards. She would hold one up and everybody would say what the answer was. Then she would hand over the flashcard to whoever got the answer the fastest. Whoever got the most flashcards won, but there was no reward. I was pretty fast at math, and Adeline once told me that she used to get mad at me for always winning. As punishment, she would give me a bunch of math problems to do. I never knew she was penalizing me. I just thought it was part of the class. So, actually, instead of getting rewarded, I got punished! But that was all right. I liked math."

Post County Line

Stuart served in the U.S. Army for three years, including two years in Germany. Once discharged he returned to Minnesota and enrolled at the Dunwoody Institute in Minneapolis where he began to pursue a career as a machinist. Following his graduation in 1963, Stuart worked at two long-lasting jobs. The first was with the 3M Company in St. Paul where he was employed for fifteen years. The second was with the Blandon Paper Company in Grand Rapids where he was employed for eighteen years, until his eventual retirement in 1995.

Stuart married Carmen Lokken, also from Thief River Falls, in 1961, and they were later blessed with three sons. During the years when their children were young, Stuart and Carmen attended a great number of youth activities in which the boys were involved. They were also kept busy hosting a long list of friends and relatives at their homes, especially their lakeside home near Grand Rapids.

Once retired Stuart began to seriously pursue a lifelong interest in music. He first honed his guitar and piano playing skills and then started performing in area dance bands, which he still does. One of the pieces he wrote and performs with his band is as follows:

The Old Country School
(Key B ♭)

Years ago when I was 5, a lunch pail hanging by my side,
I walked the road to country school each day.
In a field, far from town, farm kids came from all around
To get their ed-u-ca-tion, that way.

Outdoor toilets were the rule, in any one-room country school.
A woodshed usually was between the two.
Recess time we went to play, until we heard the teacher say,
"It's time to come in. We have work to do."

All 8 grades, just one teacher. She was the nurse; she was the preacher.
Memories still etched, in my mind.
Reading, writing, arithmetic and plays, memorization to learn each day.
An old country school, lost in time.

The wintertime we used our skis, covered up so we wouldn't freeze.
Skied across the fields to school, that way.
The teacher heated up the stove; we gathered around 'cause we were cold,
Before she started classes for the day.

Inkwell desks, chalk and blackboard, penmanship and doing flashcards.
Memories still etched, in my mind.
Books and papers, pencils, crayons, soccer balls and swings to play on.
An old country school, lost in time.
Just an old country school, called "County Line."

During the winter months, Stuart and Carmen live in the Apache Junction area of Arizona, where Stuart has also become an avid shuffleboard player.

Joyce Meyer Kron
Teacher: 1944-1946

Joyce's Memories of County Line School as Shared by October 18, 2013 Interview

(Q) How did you decide to become a teacher?

"There were a lot of influences. My grandmother was a country school teacher when she first came to Excel Township from the Goodhue area of Minnesota. She lived at home with her parents, the Simon Warrings, and she taught school near Middle River. She rode horseback from

Joyce Meyer

Excel to Middle River, kept her horse there on the farm where she boarded, and then rode back on Fridays after school. We often talked about her doing that. Then my mother became a teacher. She had gone to Steiner School, the same school as I later attended. She taught for several years before she was married.

I was never told that I should be a teacher. However, I liked school and I had one teacher, Thea Saugen, whom I very much liked. I also had another teacher, Nina Malberg, whom I very much liked. I think I decided when I had Nina that I wanted to be a teacher. Then when I went to Sunday School in Thief River Falls, I worked with children during Vacation Bible School. That was when I made up my mind for sure that I wanted to be a teacher."

(Q) *Where did you receive your training?*

"The Minnesota Department of Education had a teacher training program located in Thief River Falls. At the time I entered the teaching profession, it was located at Knox School. They provided teachers training for many years. My mother, and women teachers before her, had the same situation as I had. When they were seniors in high school, they could decide to take one more year of schooling. That would be considered normal school or, in other words, teachers training. It was a nine-month school year. A professional woman, a graduate of at least four years of college, would teach the class. She taught the rules and regulations that rural school teachers were required to follow. She also taught the principles of managing a school business, the procedure for organizing classes, and the method of teaching different subjects. We were prepared for the handiwork of going into a one-room situation.

Once hired, there were continuing education courses. The Teacher Institutes were supposed to bring us up to date. Most of us felt that it was something that was very useful. We also had professional magazines that we had to subscribe to. We were faithful in subscribing to them."

(Q) Was it difficult finding a teaching job?

"No, not for me. Back in the forties at the time I was teaching, it was getting harder for schools to find teachers because there were fewer men available to teach and women had to fill the jobs. This was because of the war efforts. The women didn't want to go too far from the area that they lived in because many of them didn't have cars. I never had a car at any time I taught school.

Clara Mae Jorde and Joyce Meyer

As the men went to the service or other war jobs, the women were left, and the wages went up because of that. So actually we were at the beginning of the raise in wages for school teachers.

In between school jobs, I once went to the Twin Cities to look for a summer job. I had the idea I would look for a war effort job. I did find some but they were not very good jobs. When fall came, I decided that my school contract was much more valuable than an inferior job in the cities. So I came back and carried out my school job and took a contract where I'd get wages in all months."

(Q) Can you describe the annual superintendent visits to the school?

"Mr. Engen was superintendent when I went to school. By the time I was teaching in Marshall County, he had decided to retire. He was there for, I think, two more years. Then Thora Skomedal was elected. She was superintendent when I was in Marshall County. Judith Lockrem was superintendent in Pennington County at that time.

On the day the superintendent visited the school, I was always concerned if she was going to be critical of something. I was concerned whether the pupils would be able to answer the questions that she might ask them. I assumed that she figured that if the questions were answered well, it was because of the teaching. There was tension. Besides looking at the room and the environment,

Joyce Meyer, upper left, with students. Front row: Janice Rood, Spencer Johnston, Stuart Solem, Philip Jaennette; back row: James Rude, Donna Rood, Muriel Copp, Dorothy Muzzy, Senora Swanson, Arlen Solem, Roger Solem

she would check out the children, their general attitude and happiness, and their response to her questions."

(Q) What was it like teaching in a one-room schoolhouse?

"Because they were all in the same room, they could listen to each other. It worked well in many ways. If they were interested, they would pay attention and would be learning beyond their age level. If they were having a hard time learning, it could be good because they were getting a review all the time from the younger children. The one disadvantage that you saw was that some children didn't get their work done, and they would have to take more work home than they would have had to."

(Q) Where did you live while you taught at County Line, and how did you get to school?

"The first year that I taught there, I stayed at Helmer Kellberg's. I only stayed there one year because they sold their farm to Ray and Florence Rausch. Rausches moved into the farm during the summer months, and I moved in with them during the fall. I stayed the first year at Kellberg's and the second year at Rausch's.

On the way to school, I walked down from the ridge, went around the barn, and then cut across the lowland to the school. I always tried to get there an hour before school, between eight and eight-thirty. I had to start the fire and warm up the building before the pupils came. I used wood. It took a while to get the room warm enough. On very cold days, we would sit around the stove and have classes because the wind chill was so great in the rest of the room."

(Q) *Was it expected of the teacher to organize a Christmas program each year?*

"Yes, Christmas programs were expected. It was a form of community entertainment. Everybody went to them. There would always be a Christmas tree. Unbelievably, we did use real candles. There would usually be school board members to stand and be recognized. We would always have treats. The school board would pay for a box or two of apples. The teacher would have to divide the peanuts into thirty, forty, or maybe fifty bags. There would always be one chocolate haystack in it, a little chocolate mound. There would be a small handful of hard candy in with the peanuts."

(Q) *On school days, what did the students do for lunch?*

"The students brought their own lunch. If they wished to heat up food in the winter, like cocoa or soup, we had an evaporating can above the stove. It had water in it at all times which got really hot. We would put their soup jars, or their container to be heated, into this evaporating can and it would be hot by dinner."

(Q) *Was there a telephone?*

"There was a telephone at County Line, but we used it only if there was a storm or something of that nature. If there was some instruction for keeping pupils or letting them go, I could call the neighbors and they could call me."

(Q) Did you have slate blackboards at County Line?

"I was very fortunate. In every school I taught in, we had slate blackboards. When I went to country school at Steiner as a student, we had slate in the front, but the blackboards on the two sidewalls were like coated linoleum. They were not easy to write on, and they did not erase well."

(Q) Besides teaching the core subjects, did you offer the students any project or activity work?

"During the last hour on Fridays, it was customary for my students to do some kind of craftwork or some kind of drama, like a little play or skit. Girls learning to sew. Boys doing some coping saw work on some wooden knick-knacks. They would usually use them as gifts for parents or somebody in the family."

Post County Line

Joyce married an area farmworker, Bert Kron, in 1946. She continued to teach at country schools for two more years and then stopped to raise a family. When all of the children were of school age, Joyce went back to school and renewed her teacher's license. By this time, however, the era of country schools was over, and Joyce worked part-time as a substitute teacher at the elementary school in Viking, Minnesota.

Joyce and Bert raised four children. When the children were young, the family enjoyed going on Sunday afternoon sightseeing excursions. The destinations were often parks located somewhere in Northwest Minnesota in which they could also picnic.

Throughout her long life, Joyce has been active in community affairs. Local organizations in which she has been especially active include Steiner and New Solum 4-H Clubs, Rosewood Homemakers, Viking Town & Country Garden Club, and the Thief River Falls United Methodist Church.

Since Bert's death in 2003, Joyce has lived at the Skylite Apartments and more recently, at the Valley Home. Both facilities are located in Thief River Falls.

6

Management and Operation

The care, management, and control of the school district was vested in three school board officers: chairman, clerk, and treasurer. The vast majority of business decisions, however, were reached collectively among the district's eligible voters during official meetings. Women had the same right of voting, signing petitions, and holding school offices as men. They also needed the same qualifications as to residence, age, and citizenship.

Annual Meetings

The official business of the school district was conducted each summer at an annual meeting held in the schoolhouse. The date was always set by the state. For the years on record, the meetings were held on the third Saturday of July from 1908 to 1924, the third Tuesday of July from 1925 to 1938, and the last Tuesday of June from 1939 to 1948.

The chairman of the schoolboard generally presided and began each meeting by asking the clerk to read the minutes of the previous year's meeting and to present the annual financial report. Attention then turned to the upcoming school year. Certain agenda items, such as the school calendar, needed to be addressed at each annual meeting. Motions were passed to set the length of the school year, as well as a starting date, a closing date, and vacation dates. County Line normally had an eight-

Clerk's record of business transacted during the July 18, 1914 annual school meeting

month school year, starting in early September and ending in late May. It generally took six weeks off at Christmas and one week off at Easter.

Providing heat for the schoolhouse was another necessary business item. Charlie Swanson was hired to supply the wood, usually five cords, for almost every year on record. Funds were always budgeted at the meetings for the wood expense and occasionally for coal and kerosene.

Since having a library was a state requirement, a motion was routinely made to continue with the traveling library. For a modest fee, Carnegie Public Library in Thief River Falls would periodically deliver books to fill the library shelves and bring back

118

others that had been there for a while. The fee was usually ten dollars a year.

Voters heard and acted on teacher recommendations. Teachers were required to make an inventory of the land (number of acres, number of shade trees, etc.), buildings, textbooks, library, and equipment at the end of each school year. For certain items, they needed to evaluate their condition as well. They were further required to make recommendations at the annual meeting based on the inventory. Voters responded, if they chose, by allocating funds for the purchase. For example, the school teacher reported in the 1936 inventory that there were eight doublewide desks and that they were in poor condition. Consequently, sufficient funds were budgeted to pay for the sixteen single desks that were purchased later in the year. At the 1937 meeting, the teacher suggested that the school should buy a telephone in order to better communicate with the students' parents. After passing a vote on the matter, the task was referred to school officials who later bought one for twenty-five dollars.

Another agenda item was the election of a school board officer. Since each of the three officers had a three-year term, and since the terms were arranged on a rotating basis, one office had to be filled each year. The polls opened at the beginning of the meeting, and the ballots were counted and the results announced near the end. The newly elected officer began his/her term at the start of the new fiscal year, which was a week or two after the election.

School Funding

The expense of operating the school was paid for almost entirely by government funding, both local and state. Motions were regularly made at annual meetings for the district to raise a certain amount of money to help meet the school's financial needs. The amount was forwarded to the offices of both county auditors who used it as a guide for levying a maintenance tax among the residents of the district. The revenue raised was returned to the district in three annual payments.

The school received additional operating money from the state. Included was a variety of state aid that was designated for specific uses such as library, transportation, and supplemental. Also included was an apportionment of state funds that came mainly from fines and penalties. The state sent the funding to the counties, which in turn, allocated the money to the district.

Treasurer's Report for the 1918-19 school year

Special Meetings

If there was a pressing need, a special meeting could be called at any time of the year. In November of 1913, the district held a special meeting in which they voted against uniting with the Thief River Falls School District; in July of 1919, the district held a special meeting in which they voted in favor of building an eight by eighteen foot shed; and in July of 1926, they held a special meeting in which voters decided to raise three hundred dollars to transport their pupils to the North Star School for the next school year. Throughout its history, though, County Line held very few special meetings.

Other

Certain decisions, such as hiring teachers, were left for the school board. Most of the teachers hired were young girls from the area who had attended the Thief River Falls Teacher Training Program. They, in turn, took on certain daily chores such as starting the heating stove in the morning before the students arrived and sweeping the floor in the afternoon after they left. Repair and maintenance jobs were generally carried out by neighbors who were hired to paint the buildings, shingle the roofs, scrub the floors, and a variety of other tasks. There were years in which the teachers were expected to do the scrubbing as part of their contract. Some years they were paid extra, and and some years they were not.

Teacher's Contract.

This Agreement, Made this 25th _____ day of July _____ 19 20
between School District No. 219 - 72 in the County of Penn & Marshall State of
Minnesota, by the School Board, at a meeting called for that purpose* _____

and Miss Gunda Engen a legally qualified teacher.

WITNESSETH, That the said Gunda Engen shall teach the school in said
district for the term of 8 months, for the sum of 100 00 Dollars
per month, commencing on the 7th day of September 19 20
And the said Gunda Engen agrees faithfully to teach the said school according
to the best of her ability, and to keep a register of the daily attendance of each pupil belonging to
the school, and make such report of the school as is or may be required by law or by the County
Superintendent, or by the State Superintendent of Public Instruction, and to observe and enforce all
rules and regulations established by proper authority for the government and management of said
school, and use her best endeavors to preserve in good condition the school house and premises
connected with it, also the apparatus and furniture thereto belonging, and also all books and records
provided by the School Board for the use of said school, and to deliver the same to the clerk of said
district at the close of said term of school in as good condition as when received, natural wear and
tear excepted. The said School Board hereby agrees to keep the school house and premises in good
repair, provide suitable and sufficient fuel prepared for fire, and to supply the following articles as
described, for the school room : _____

It is Further Agreed, Between the School Board and the said teacher:

FIRST.—In respect to janitor work, including the building of fires, sweeping and keeping the school
room clean : That said Miss Gunda Engen
agrees to do the Janitor work free of
any additional charge

SECOND —With respect to vacations during the school year : Vacation of
6 weeks during January and half of
February

The district also agrees to pay the said Miss Gunda Engen for the
above described services the sum of 800.00 dollars
in monthly payments of 100 00
each Month. _____ Dollars

In Witness whereof, We have hereunto subscribed our names this Twenty-fifth
day of July 19 20 Pennington
School District No. 219 & 72 Marshall County, Minn.
Hugh Best Chairman.
By { _____ Treasurer.
Peter Solem Clerk.
Gunda Engen Teacher.

*Note.—If the contract is with a teacher related by blood or marriage to any member of the School Board, add after the *
in the above form the words, "with the concurrence of all the members thereof by vote duly entered on the clerk's record of
proceedings."

[SIGN IN DUPLICATE]

The duplicate should be a copy of the above made when the contract is signed. Such copy should be also signed by all the
parties signing the above. It should be taken and preserved by the teacher for proof and for reference.
The teacher is not required to teach school on January 1st, February 12th, February 22nd, Good Friday, Memorial
Day, July 4th, the first Monday in September (Labor Day), the Tuesday next after the first Monday in November in
even numbered years (General Election Day), Thanksgiving Day, or Christmas Day, and no deduction from the teacher's
time or wages can be made when a school day happens to be one of these days.

Teacher's Contract for the 1920-21 school year

War Efforts

Like millions of other school children across the country, County Line students participated in the war efforts of both world wars. When our soldiers went off to fight during World War I, there was a conviction among those left at home that everyone needed to contribute in the war effort, including children. As a result, the American Junior Red Cross was created in 1917, mainly to provide a way for school children to do their part.

World War I

Throughout America students became members of the Junior Red Cross. Their schools served as auxiliaries, and it cost twenty-five cents to join. In February of 1918, the Pennington County Superintendent of Schools sent out a patriotic plea for all of the schools in his county to become auxiliaries of the Junior Red Cross.

> To the children of Pennington County rural schools:
> Dear children,
> As you know, this nation is now at war and our Uncle Sam is in sore distress, for he carries heavy burdens for you and me and for all men and women in the whole land. Our Uncle is surely a very dear old chap in thus looking after our well-being,

and if he does double up his fist, it is because some nation or some countries are trying to steal a move on us to do us harm, but the watchful eye of our Uncle Sam is upon them, and we trust that our lives and your rights as little citizens of this country shall not be taken away from us. But because our enemies are thus threatening us, therefore the dear old Uncle is in sore trouble and as we are the loyal children we are troubled too and we must assist our Uncle in withstanding the attack upon our rights as citizens of this great country and as children of Uncle Sam. The venerable Uncle is full of vigor and fighting force. But strong as he may be, he is but one whereas of us school children, there are twenty-two million scattered all over this magnificent land given Uncle Sam and his children to protect. What can we not do for Uncle even as pupils in our common schools when we are united in purpose and action in the defense of our rights.

Now let me tell you dear children, that our Uncle Sam, that is, our country which we are proud to name the United States of America, of whom President Wilson is at this moment the great leader, is asking us to do a great deal to win this war, this fight for our rights and liberties.

Someone, probably a brother of yours, has been asked to do much and has now left your companionship and home, left father and mother to go to the front and is now doing a valiant fight and suffering much hardship in order that we at home now and those millions of school children of the future in our country shall enjoy the sweet blessings of a free country. At some time, too, some of the sisters in the neighborhood will find it their duty to go to the assistance of Uncle Sam in caring for the wounded and the bleeding in the battlefield. Now then, the question is what can we do, what can you do, pupils of Pennington County? This is what you can do, and which must be done in every school district in Pennington County before Feb. 22 inclusive:

1. To organize a Junior Red Cross Auxiliary
2. To enroll therein every member of the school
3. To pledge the support of each member of the school to do some Red Cross work for the help of the soldiers in the field
4. To pay a fee, a sum of money, by the school to the Red Cross Fund equal to 25 cents for each enrolled member or pupil in the school

The money thus raised will go to buy material for the Junior Red Cross Auxiliary. None of this money goes to defray the expenses of the fraternal organization or the county chapter organization of the Red Cross.

The thing to do first is to organize at the very earliest moment. The teacher will be chairman of the Junior Auxiliary of the school and direct all activities. Committees may be appointed to assist in the work.

Now, dear children, Columbia is crying and in sorrow; our hearts feel sad for what has happened. Let us then be up and doing with a heart for any fate in this national crisis and let us show, by the hearty support of this Red Cross movement, that we are loyal subjects of Uncle Sam; that we feel for the men on the battle front by doing "our bit" to help them in this hour of need. Let us, as Lincoln said in the Gettysburg speech, "Rather be dedicated" to the fullest degree in the noble activities essential to win in this dreaded conflict the fight for a free government. I trust, in fact I know, you will do your part.

Respectfully submitted,
E. A. Mostue, County Superintendent of Schools, Thief River Falls[67]

County Line School complied with the superintendent's request. On March 1, 1918, the school held a patriotic program at the schoolhouse and charged a twenty-five cent admission fee to pay for the Junior Red Cross memberships. As was the case across America, each student that joined was awarded a membership pin to wear.

"The children in the County Line School gave a patriotic program at County Line schoolhouse last Friday evening. At the close of the program, lunch was served. An admission of twenty-five cents was charged. The proceeds went to the Red Cross. A large crowd was present and a merry time was reported."[68]

While it is not known for certain what type of Red Cross work the County Line students participated in, one can assume it was similar to that performed by students everywhere in the country. Among other activities, school children held fundraisers; collected throwaway items such as old clothes and papers; and knitted and sewed items of clothing such as socks, sweaters, and wristlets.

A popular method of fundraising was the selling of war savings stamps. War savings stamps were interest bearing, and the owners could redeem them at a profit on their maturity date. If a person couldn't afford one, thrift stamps were offered at a far less expensive price. Thrift stamps were not interest bearing but could be accumulated until the investment added up to the cost of a war savings stamp and then be exchanged.

Because every neighborhood had a schoolhouse, schools were often used as sites for selling war savings stamps. In Marshall County, the clerk of every school district was assigned to be in charge of their sales. It was explained in an article that appeared in the *Warren Sheaf* on March 6, 1918:

W.F. Powell, Chairman of the War Savings Committee of Marshall County reports that the organization has been extended so as to reach every person in Marshall County. The clerk in each school district in the county has been placed in charge of the sales of War Savings and Thrift Stamps in his district and sales agencies have been established at each schoolhouse where the stamps may be secured. It is the duty of every citizen – boys and girls included – to economize, save, and invest.[69]

At the annual Teachers' Institute held in Warren during September of 1918, the delegates voted in favor of establishing a Teachers' Patriotic League. As a result of the vote, every teacher in the county was expected to organize a Little Citizens' League at his/her school, and every student in the county was expected to join the league and carry out the war work and other patriotic activities as directed by his/her teacher. These expectations were described in an article that appeared in the *Warren Sheaf* on September 18, 1918:

> The Teachers' Patriotic League expects to cooperate with the other county organizations and to carry on systematic patriotic work. Every school in the county is expected to be organized into a Little Citizens' League and through it accomplish school improvement, school war work, and train for actual patriotic service.[70]

The action taken at the conference was in response to a request from the State Department of Education. During the summer of 1918, the department had distributed a lengthy instructional book entitled *School Patriotism: Hand Book for Teachers' Patriotic League and Little Citizens' League* to every county superintendent in the state. The handbook, which was compiled by the state superintendent, was to be used as a guide for organizing and carrying out the activities of the two leagues.[71]

"Utensil Demonstration"
(One of a host of suggested activities for the Little Citizens' League.)

Girls in cooking uniform each carrying utensil appropriate to their lines.

First girl:	*CAN* the Kaiser.
Second girl:	*WHIP* the Whiner.
Third girl:	*WHIP* the slacker, too.
Fourth girl:	*ROAST* the pacifist.
Fifth girl:	*DRAIN* our purses dry.
Sixth girl:	*MEASURE* justice to your neighbor.
Seventh girl:	*BAKE* corn meal and rye.
Eighth girl:	*SKIM* the totals of your bank book.
Ninth girl:	*SMALL FRY* can help, too.
Tenth girl:	*CHOP* excuses out entirely.
Eleventh girl:	*CUT* expenses in two.
ALL:	*BUY* a Liberty Bond.[72]

On November 11, 1918, only two months after the Marshall County Teachers' Institute ended, World War I ended as well. Although the fighting had stopped, the patriotic fervor that was gained during the war continued, and both the Teachers' Patriotic League and the Little Citizens' League continued to function. Eventually, the Teachers' Patriotic League evolved into the Marshall County Teachers' Association.

World War II

The peace did not last long. In 1939 basically the same two sides renewed the struggle. When the United States entered the Second World War in December of 1941, County Line students were quick to join a second student war effort.

What is known about the school's involvement in WWII comes largely from a student log that was issued during the 1942-43 school year (Note: An abbreviated version of the log appears in the appendix of this book). The log, which was distributed semimonthly among the students' families, shows that their participation was similar to that of WWI students. As in the first war, the students joined the American Junior Red Cross, made items of clothing, collected scrap, and sold war savings stamps. The log also reveals that the Citizens' League was still functioning. It was now called the Junior Citizens' League.

In 1942 the War Production Board launched a nationwide campaign to salvage scrap. When President Franklin Roosevelt sent out an official letter asking children to enter into scrap drives, County Line students responded by forming a Junior Scrap Army. The effort, which was organized by their teacher Bernice Halvorson, was arranged along military lines. The students scoured the neighborhood looking for different kinds of scrap, especially metal which could be melted down and reshaped to make guns, bullets, jeeps, and so forth. The following quote is taken from the October 16, 1942 issue of the *County Line Log*:

Bernice Halvorson

All over the United States the pupils of all the schools have started a Junior Scrap Army. Our slogan is "Save Scrap to Lick a Jap." Our officers and their duties are: Captain, Miss Halvorson - to assign places and arranging transportation of the scrap; Lieutenant, Kenneth Arras - to keep the books; Sergeant, Lowell Rude - to weigh the scrap and fix boxes for tinfoil, brass, and so on; Corporal, James Arras - to sort the scrap.[73]

Similar to the WWI effort, the students sold war savings stamps to help pay for the war. The stamps from WWII could be purchased for as little as ten cents, but they did not earn interest as they did in the first war. What the buyers could do, however, was to accumulate them in collection booklets to be used later for purchasing war bonds. The amount of weekly sales was publicized in each student log.

During the war, students across America changed the way in which they delivered the Pledge of Allegiance. Instead of extending their right arm towards the flag during its delivery, they kept their right hand covering their heart. The change was noted in the March 26, 1943 issue of the *County Line Log*.

> There is a new way to salute the flag. Instead of raising your hand toward the flag when you say, "to the flag," you leave it on your chest while saying the entire pledge. The reason for this change is that when the Germans say, "Heil Hitler," they raise their hand, and our former way of saluting reminded some people of this.[74]

The salute was known as the Bellamy Salute, after Francis Bellamy who had authored the pledge during the 1890s. When a similar salute began to be used by the Italian fascists and German Nazis during the 1920s and 30s, many Americans became uneasy with its use here at home. The concern peaked after the United States entered WWII to fight against Italy and Germany, and it resulted in the salute being changed by Congress on December 22, 1942.

On August 15, 1945, three months after the surrender of the Axis forces in Europe, Japan surrendered as well, and WWII was finished.

Patriotism

Patriotism played an important role in the daily lives of County Line students. The American flag flew from a pole on the east side of the schoolhouse, and each school day began by reciting the Pledge of Allegiance. On Armistice Day, it was a tradition to honor the soldiers who had died during WWI by stopping the daily routine at exactly 11:00 a.m., standing, and facing the east for a minute of silence. Eleven o'clock was the time of the day that the armistice became effective, and east is the direction from the school where the war was fought.

Most of the County Line students also participated in patriotic activities away from the school. Many of them joined either the 4-H or Scouts, and a few joined both programs. At the onset of each regular meeting, the members of both youth organizations were required to recite a pledge that, among other promises, promised their patriotism.

Arlen Solem was a second-grade student at County Line during the 1943-44 school year. At the school's fall carnival on October 15, 1943, he delivered the following recitation:

Arlen Solem, 8th Grade

Columbus found America in 1492.
They teach that to us here in school,
And so I know it's true.
Now we must save America in 1943,
So they can teach in future days
That we have kept it free.[75]

Arlen and the other County Line students realized the significance of their war efforts, and their involvement had a lasting influence on their lives. After the war, they continued to be thrifty by "economizing, saving, and investing." They also continued to be of service to their country, their communities, and others in need.

Arlen joined the U.S. Army in January of 1957. He was later stationed at the Dugway Proving Ground in Dugway, Utah, where he served as the company clerk for his unit. While there, he was shot and killed by an arrow in a tragic hunting accident. He was 21 years old at the time of his death on September 4, 1958.

PFC (E-3) Arlen Solem

8

Consolidation

By the late 1940s, country schools across the nation, including Minnesota, were struggling to survive. Most of them had experienced a significant drop in enrollment numbers, and the trend was expected to continue. Therefore, a loud cry to consolidate could be heard everywhere.

This chapter chronicles the history of school consolidation in Minnesota from the 1890s through the 1940s. In the process, it follows the ongoing battle waged by family farmers to save their beloved neighborhood schools. The chapter also follows the mandatory school reorganization efforts that took place in Pennington and Marshall Counties after the Minnesota State Legislature passed a crucial school consolidation bill in 1947.

The Number of School Districts Soars

When Minnesota became a state in 1858, its population was very low, and there was little need for many schools. That situation soon changed after the United States Congress passed the Homestead Act of 1862. The act offered prospective settlers one hundred and sixty acres of free federal land in exchange for meeting certain requirements. Minnesota was widely known for its abundance of fertile land, and homesteaders flocked to the state.

Once settled, schools were organized for the children. Most students needed to walk to school, and since parents didn't want their children walking for more than two or three miles, an enormous number of schools were necessary. Consequently, neighborhoods petitioned their county governments to start more and more districts. According to a study done by the Department of Education, there were approximately eight thousand school districts in Minnesota by 1900,[76] the vast majority of which were rural districts with only one school.

Professional Educators and Farmers Clash Over School Reorganization

A popular belief among professional educators was that the number of schools was too high, and the state needed to change the way districts were being organized. They felt a change was necessary in order to make schools more efficient to operate and equal for its students. Many of them viewed centralization as the solution and advocated going back to the township system.

Farmers, meanwhile, insisted on keeping their neighborhood schools. As stated in the book *The Old Country School: The Story of Rural Education in the Middle West*, they were "opposed to centralization, unwilling to give up the control of their schools and their right to tax themselves for education, and deeply committed to the principle of self-help."[77] It was farmers who led the fight against reorganization.

Prior to the 1895 legislative session, county commissioners in Minnesota were requested to voice their opinions on whether or not the state should return to the township system. The state superintendent was in favor of the change, and the legislative leaders wanted to find out where the commissioners stood on the issue. Just three days after they organized School District No. 72-219J (County Line), the Polk County Board of County Commissioners passed the following resolution:

> Whereas the matter of changing the present school system of our state into what is known as the township system of school districts is likely to come up before the present session of the state legislature for consideration, and an expression of our opinion being requested of the county board. Therefore be it resolved, that the board of county commissioners of Polk County are unanimously opposed to such proposed change, and are in favor of the present system for the reasons that it is more just and equitable to taxpayers, and more convenient for school children, teachers, and conducive to much better schools.
>
> J.E. Oppegaard
> M.E. Kirsch
> Anton Lindem
> Henry Norland
> County Commissioners
> Dated at Crookston, Minn. Jan. 11th, 1895[78]

The legislature apparently agreed with the Polk County commissioners and decided to keep the neighborhood plan intact. As the years passed, professional educators and farmers continued to clash on the issue. Due to the large number of farmers in the state, farmers usually won the battles. State superintendents who advocated systemic change, on the other hand, often had a short stay in office.

Early Legislation

An early advocate for school reorganization was Gov. A.O. Eberhart, who served as governor of Minnesota from 1909-1915. He was a product of a one-room country school, and he held an extremely negative view of them. It was written about him that, "He feelingly recalled the old school with its little one room building, bare walls, benches, wooden bucket and dipper, its narrow course of inferior teaching, its unattractive and unsanitary construction, and pleaded with the legislature for state aid to encourage consolidation."[79]

Largely due to Eberhart's efforts, the legislature passed a bill in 1911 that offered financial incentives to newly consolidated districts. The state agreed to pick up one-fourth of the cost for a new building and also provide annual aid up to fifteen hundred dollars "if the school met eight months of the year and supplied transportation for pupils living long distances from the school building."[80]

Obstacles to Consolidation

The new legislation didn't make much of an impact. Farmers remained opposed to consolidation for a variety of reasons. They were concerned that consolidation would lead to higher taxes, and that the tax burden would fall disproportionately on them. They also disliked relinquishing local control over their children's education and were worried about destroying an institution that held rural communities together.

Another roadblock was the lack of suitable transportation that existed in 1911. Motorized vehicles were just beginning to appear on the scene, and the roads in rural areas were primitive. Using horse drawn buses and sleighs to transport children for long distances seemed unsafe and impractical.

By 1930 the number of school districts using motorized buses had significantly increased, but mainly in urban areas. Buses weren't yet dependable to operate during the coldest months of winter, and many of the side roads remained impassable for much of the year. Consequently, rural districts were still hesitant about their usefulness.

The Thief River Falls School District (now identified as District No.18) purchased its first motorized bus during the 1929-30 school year. Prior to that time, only horse drawn buses and sleighs had been used to transport students. While the new "motor bus" was helpful, the district couldn't depend solely on its use as the following piece indicates:

> Mr. Taylor began transporting children on Route No. 3 on December 18 using the bus and sleigh that we had on hand which has been used on Route No. 1.
>
> The Maintenance Committee has purchased from the Sandeen Garage a Ford motor bus at a cost of $400.00 to be used on this route. So far Mr. Taylor has been using the sleigh, as the weather has been tremendously cold, and we have not been able to find any satisfactory heater to be installed in

the bus. Furthermore, Mr. Taylor tells me there is one spot on that route which would be impassable by car whenever there is a snowstorm, so possibly for the present month it would be advisable not to attempt to use the motor bus.[81]

In addition to taxes and transportation, there were other obstacles to consolidation as well. Between 1914 and 1945, Americans were preoccupied with two world wars and a terrible depression. Consequently, by the 1943-44 school year, there were still close to seventy-seven hundred school districts in Minnesota,[82] very few of which had both an elementary and a high school. According to a Marshall County publication:

> By 1944 there were ten states in which every school district included both an elementary school and a high school. On the other hand, there were only five states, of which Minnesota was one, with less than 10% of districts in a high school organization. Minnesota had the dubious honor of having the lowest (5.95) percentage of all 48 states.[83]

Consolidation Becomes a Priority for the State Legislature

It wasn't until the late forties and early fifties that conditions were ready for a massive consolidation. Accelerated urbanization had drastically reduced the number of students available for funding rural schools, our country was experiencing an extensive period of peace and prosperity, and the means of travel had significantly improved. Rural children no longer needed to walk or travel by horse to get to a school. Large dependable motorized buses were available for transporting students on improved and well-maintained roads. While farmers dreaded the thought of losing their neighborhood schools, low enrollment numbers had made the cost of maintaining them prohibitive.

In 1947 the consolidation of school districts became a priority for the Minnesota State Legislature. Among other legislative actions, lawmakers passed a bill to eliminate a provision that "granted free high school tuition to children living outside a district operating a high school."[84] The new legislation removed an important financial incentive that had previously discouraged rural schools from consolidating.

County Survey Committees

State legislators passed a second bill in 1947 that may have had an even greater impact. The bill provided for the appointment of a State Advisory Commission on School Reorganization by the State Board of Education. It also set up survey committees in every county of the state. The intent was to have the Advisory Commission coordinate a statewide effort to promote school consolidation involving itself, the county survey committees, the State Board of Education, and the state legislature. Their task was to reorganize the school districts within each county in order to "provide a more efficient and economical basis for equalizing educational opportunity."[85]

With guidance from the State Advisory Commission, each county survey committee was required to come up with a list of recommendations to be brought to the voters in a referendum. The committees were given strict deadlines to meet. Tentative recommendations were due by September 1, 1948; final recommendations were due by November 1, 1948; and then the final recommendations needed to be submitted to the voters within nine months in a referendum.

Farmers Express Fear

The survey committees sought community involvement by holding public forums. The meetings were often emotional and sometimes volatile. Much of the criticism came from farmers who continued to express fear. Among other concerns, they were fearful of sending their young children on long bus rides and fearful of losing local control of their schools. They wanted to keep farm children in their own neighborhoods with people they knew and trusted. Some of them thought that the state was forcing consolidation on them and were angry. Others in attendance, however, favored consolidation and welcomed it as progress. It was a highly divisive issue.

The anger expressed was generally directed at the State Department, and it occasionally led to acts of lawlessness. Mary Drees, Red Lake County Superintendent of Schools from 1947 to 1967, in the county directly to the south of Pennington, shared the following story while writing about her years as superintendent:

> "This is one extreme case that happened my first year in office. Since Red Lake County was so small and way up north from the State Department,

we were being pushed into consolidation. They had made a date with Oklee to call for an election of thirteen districts to join Oklee School. So I went to Oklee on the night the election was to be voted on in the City Hall. This was all done by the State Department. It had rained for a couple of days and was raining very hard that night. There was only one track in front of the hall because it was so deep in mud. People came and were voting on whether they would join together or not. All at once some men came in, threw the ballot box out in the mud and continued on over to Oklee School. They broke windows and threw tomatoes and eggs all over my car, the hall, and school. One of the men called the police. We took the box to the printing office where the count was recorded and sent to the Cities to the State Department of Education. I had my shoes and socks off and was covered with mud. The cop and I were also soaking wet. There wasn't anyplace to drive as all streets were blocked. Such a night! Then I woke up to a telephone call from Mr. Sorvig, County Superintendent of Polk County schools. He said he was going to have me in jail by nighttime for forcing one of the joint districts into Oklee. I just listened and was scared to death. I went to the Court House and contacted our County Attorney, Mr. C. Boughton. He said, "You did only what the State Department had planned to do." So by noon hour the State Department told Mr. Sorvig to apologize or he would be out of his position. He did. The Oklee School was a much better school in the years that followed. Many other districts couldn't keep up so they joined, little by little, either Plummer, Red Lake Falls, Mentor, Erskine, or Thief River Falls – whichever bus line was the closest." [86]

Marshall and Pennington Counties Work to Complete Survey Reports

The Marshall County School Survey Committee submitted its final report before the November 1, 1948, deadline. At the time, the county had one hundred and thirty-seven school districts, plus some unorganized districts. The committee's proposal was to consolidate the vast majority of the districts into seventeen administrative units and to leave thirty school districts "unassigned for the present."[87] The report was critical of the lack of time given to the committee to complete its work stating that "the resurvey movement was moving too rapidly for the general public to become properly informed concerning the merits of the plan and voted to partially redistrict the county leaving 30 common school districts unassigned." [88] County Line was one of the thirty unassigned districts.

The Pennington County committee, meanwhile, sent their tentative recommendations to the state before the September 1, 1948 deadline but never submitted a final report. Their tentative proposal was to consolidate the majority of the districts into eleven administrative units and to leave eleven individual districts as they were. In this plan, County Line was to be consolidated with the Thief River Falls School District.[89] As for the final report, the committee apparently followed the advice of the Thief River Falls Times editor who, in an editorial published less than two weeks before the deadline, urged the committee to "conclude its work for the time being" and conduct "further studies":

> At several meetings of citizens called by the county school survey committee during the past week for the purpose of determining public reactions to the committee's proposals for school district reorganization, it has been evident that not sufficient time is provided under the present law to properly present so involved a program. The law requires that a final report, with specific recommendations for district reorganization be completed by November first, and that these proposals for consolidation and reorganization be submitted to the voters for approval or rejection within nine months. With the first of November little more than a week away, it would be impossible to prepare a reasonably satisfactory program of reorganization for this county.
>
> This seems to be the situation generally throughout the state and it is practically certain that the time limit will be extended or removed entirely by the legislature when it convenes this winter. In view of this probability, it would not be out of order for the committee to conclude its work for the time being by recommending that further studies be made of the problem.[90]

As predicted in the editorial, the 1949 legislature extended the deadlines, and the state's endeavor to reorganize its school districts was delayed. There were counties, however, where the process swiftly moved forward. In Marshall County, several referendums were held during 1949, and many of them passed.

The District Ends

Primarily due to declining enrollment, County Line was forced to close its doors for the 1949-50 school year. Most residents of the district clung to the idea that the shutdown was temporary, and that the school would reopen after a year or two. It would never happen.

Past Shutdowns

The school had been temporarily shut down twice before. During the 1926-27 school year, the district transported its students to the North Star School located in Pennington County. It was part of a two-year reciprocal agreement in which the County Line District agreed to send its students to North Star for the first year, provided that the North Star District would send its students to County Line for the second. The next shutdown occurred during the 1929-30 and 1930-31 school years when the district sent its students to the Steiner School located in Marshall County. During both closures, the district paid for the students' transportation and tuition as required by law.

The two shutdowns had been the result of low student enrollment. County Line went through a six-year period from 1925 to 1931 in which they averaged only five students per year. When the numbers sufficiently recovered, the school reopened its doors.

Growing Concerns

Enrollment was significantly down again for the 1949-50 school year. The Mattson family had moved outside of the school district, and Muriel Copp had graduated. It was left with only six students. Consequently, the district decided to close the school for a year. Arlen, Roger, and Stuart Solem went to Steiner; Philip and Carol Jaennette, along with Gary Mason, attended school in Thief River Falls.

At the annual meeting for the 1950-51 school year, residents of the district were faced with an even more difficult decision — whether or not to permanently close the school. Student numbers remained at six, and future projections were even lower. They could either reopen the school, continue transporting their students to other schools, or petition to dissolve their district and consolidate with another. Times were rapidly changing, and rural schools were experiencing difficulties all across the country. And as the gathering discussed the school's future, it became apparent that declining enrollment wasn't the only obstacle it faced.

In 1947 high school tuition policies had changed for Minnesota schools. It was no longer tuition free for graduates of an eight-year country school to attend a high school located outside of their district.[91] This meant that County Line graduates could no longer attend Lincoln High School in Thief River Falls free of charge. Under the new policy, the cost of instruction was passed on to the landowners of their district by an increase in property tax. In 1947, for example, Marshall County had a tax rate of 7.44 mills[92] and Pennington County a rate of 15 mills[93] that was uniformly spread out among the school districts in their counties without a high school (one mill is equal to $1 in property tax levied per $1,000 of a property's assessed value).

State standards requiring an approved well was another issue discussed. The State Board of Education was putting increased pressure on the district to upgrade the well, which was alkaline and could not be used. If it didn't comply, the State Board was threatening to withhold all of the special state aids.

A growing concern was finding qualified teachers. Largely due to World War II, there was a serious teacher shortage throughout the United States. Rural schools were especially hard hit. Pay was higher and working conditions were better in the cities, and improvements in transportation made it easier for teachers to travel longer distances to work.

Among the options offered at the annual meeting was consolidation. In June two County Line officials, Ray Rausch and Edwin Swanson, had appeared before the Thief River Falls School Board to explore the possibility of a consolidation.[94] While few in the district liked the idea, it had become a practical solution for many.

School Board Overrides Vote

After hearing the arguments presented during the meeting, County Line residents took a vote. A motion to reopen the school passed by a single vote. However, since there were lingering concerns over questions that no one present was able to answer, Alfred Solem was chosen to draft a letter to the State Department of Education in Saint Paul. The following letter is a response from the state to those questions:

July 10, 1950
Mr. Alfred Solem
Route 2
Thief River Falls, Minnesota

Dear Mr. Solem:

Your letter addressed to the State Department of Education was given to me to answer. It seems that you have a number of problems in your school district. I will attempt to answer the questions in the order in which you asked them.

At the annual meeting or a legally called special meeting, the voters have the right to vote on the question of closing a school or reopening it. The school board, however, must make the final decision. Even though the voters by one vote were in favor of reopening the school in your district, your school board by majority vote can close it and transport the children to Thief River Falls.

When the school has been closed, the school board must furnish transportation and instruction. The school board has the legal authority to designate one school and one bus driver or more than one school and more than one bus driver. There must be a contract for instruction and a contract for transportation. These contracts must be drawn in accordance with the laws of Minnesota and the regulations of the State Board of Education. Contract blanks for this purpose can be secured from your county superintendent of schools, Mrs. Martha Matheson.

If a school is maintained, it must be up to the standards prescribed by the State Board of Education. That is, all of the provisions for maintaining a school given in the "Manual for Ungraded Elementary Schools" on pages 7 to 19 must be met, or the State Board of Education may withhold all of the special state aids. The school building must meet the requirements given in the "Manual for Ungraded Elementary Schools." There must be an approved well on the school site. The pump and other facilities used in connection with the water supply must meet the requirements of the State Department of Health. During these times when it is difficult to secure qualified teachers for the elementary grades, it doesn't seem reasonable to reopen a school. On the other hand, there isn't any law or regulation of the State Board of Education that provides for a minimum number of children in an elementary school.

At the annual meeting each question must be clearly submitted to the voters. It isn't proper or legal to combine several questions such as closing the school, providing transportation and consolidation on one ballot. The matter of closing the school is one separate and distinct question. The matter of having a school district dissolved is also a separate matter and must be taken up by the voters in a definite, clear-cut manner. The law in regard to closing a school is Section 125.14.

If you have any further questions in regard to this matter, please feel free to call on us.

Very truly yours,
Roy H. Larson
Ass't Director of Rural Education[95]

After reviewing the state department letter, the school board decided to override the vote, close the school for another year, and continue transporting its students to other districts. Roger, Stuart, and Kathryn Solem, along with Robert Rausch, went to Steiner School; Philip and Carol Jaennette continued going to Knox School in Thief River Falls. The board also decided to pursue the process of dissolution.

District No. 72-219J Petitions to Dissolve

On February 27, 1951, County Line School Board members filed a petition with the Pennington County auditor's office to dissolve School District No. 72-219J and have it annexed to the Thief River Falls School District (District No. 18). The reason given for filing the petition was, "That there will be only five pupils attending for some time to come, and it will be impossible to operate efficiently." Nineteen residents of the school district signed the petition.[96]

A few days later, a spokesperson presented the petition to the Pennington County Board of County Commissioners who granted a hearing for 2 p.m. on April 3rd.[97] The petition was also presented to the Marshall County Board of County Commissioners, and they arranged a hearing for 11 a.m. on April 3rd.[98]

Six days prior to the April hearings, the Thief River Falls School Board held a special meeting to discuss the County Line petition, and they decided to make a request for a postponement until after the adjournment of the Minnesota State Legislature. A delay was necessary, they felt, in order to provide the legislature with more time to clarify its pending legislation on school taxation.[99] Consequently, Marshall County set a new hearing for June 5th at 10 a.m.,[100] and Pennington County set one for June 5th at 2 p.m.[101]

The Thief River Falls School Board had concerns other than school taxation as well. They knew of more struggling schools in the area and were concerned about having adequate "facilities for taking care of additional pupils" and with "the matter of what the ultimate aim of Independent School District No. 18 should be in regard to increase of size."[102] If the Thief River Falls School District was going to eventually annex not only County Line but several of the surrounding country schools, it felt it needed to be thoroughly prepared.

Petition Denied

During the 1951 legislative session, a bill was passed that "provided for the dissolution of some 'closed' school districts."[103] A "closed" school district was a district that no longer operated a school but rather transported its students to another district. The new legislation allowed districts that hadn't operated a school for two years to be dissolved by any of three methods: one, the county commissioners could do it on their own; two, the voters of a school district could do it by a majority vote of those present at a legal meeting; or three, it could be done on a petition signed by a majority of the voters in a school district.[104]

The new legislation made it easier for closed districts such as County Line to be dissolved. However, there still was a potential snag in the process. Before a district could be dissolved, another district needed to be willing to annex it.

At the June 5th morning hearing held in Warren, the Marshall County commissioners declined to act on the petition. It was recorded in the minutes that they wanted to wait and see how the Pennington County commissioners would react to the arguments.[105] Later that same day, the Pennington County commissioners voted to deny the petition because an "objection was made to the annexation."[106]

Waiting for Consolidation

With the petition to dissolve having been denied, the County Line District decided to continue transporting its students for the 1951-52 school year. This time all of the students attended school in Thief River Falls. It started a pattern that continued into the 1955-56 school year. Each fall district officials drew up two contracts with the Thief River Falls District. One dealt with the cost of instruction and was called a Closed School Contract. The other one dealt with the cost of transportation and was called a Transportation Service Contract.

154

The Public Schools
Thief River Falls, Minnesota

State of Minnesota
Department of Education

TRANSPORTATION SERVICE CONTRACT

THIS AGREEMENT, Made this ____1st____ day of ____August____, 19_49_

between the School Board of District No. 219J, County of ___Pennington___

State of Minnesota, the party of the first part paying for the trans-

portation, and the School Board of Independent School District No. 18,

County of Pennington, State of Minnesota, the party of the second part

furnishing the transportation service,

WITNESSETH, That the said party of the second part agrees to
furnish transportation service for the high school children of the
party of the first part, from the nearest station on the bus route to
the school building located in School District No. 18, County of
Pennington, and return for every day that school is in session during
the school year of 1949 - 1950, providing the roads are passable, and
providing further that such bus route shall be located entirely within
the local high school area. The party of the second part agrees to
furnish transportation equipment which meets with the legal requirements and to provide a licensed and qualified driver to operate such
equipment, and agrees that such transportation service shall be in
accordance with the rules and regulations adopted by the State Board
of Education and the Commissioner of Highways and set forth in bulle-
tins of the State Department of Education, Code VII-B-41 and VII-B-42.

It is further agreed that the said children will meet the school
bus at the designated station on the route at the time specified on
the schedule.

It is further agreed that a pupil must be absent for a full month
before receiving any reduction.

NOW, THEREFORE, In consideration for such services, the party of
the first part agrees to pay the party of the second part, the sum of
_____$8.00_____ per pupil per month, and such payment
is to be made on ___January 21, 1950,___ and ___June 10, 1950___ .

In WITNESS WHEREOF, We have hereunto subscribed our hands this
__5__ day of __August__, 19_49_.

Party of First Part: Party of Second Part:

School District No. _219J_   School District No. __18__
County of _Pennington_, Minn.   County of __Pennington__ Minn.

By _Ray Rausch_ Chairman   By _Otis A Wold_ Chairman
Mrs. Alfred Solem Clerk   _L H Semes_ Clerk

Transportation Service Contract with School District 18

155

CLOSED SCHOOL CONTRACT
Instruction and/or Transportation

THIS AGREEMENT made this __25__ day of __August__, 19_49_, between School District No. _219J_ in the County of __Pennington__ and the State of Minnesota, by the School Board of said District party of the first part (district with closed school), and School District No. _18_ in the County of __Pennington__ and the State of Minnesota by the School Board of said District party of the second part (district providing the services).

WITNESSETH That the said party of the second part agrees to furnish in accordance with provisions and requirements of the Laws of Minnesota and the regulations of the State Board of Education, the services and equipment as indicated below during the entire school year ending __June 2__, 19_50_, for consideration of and at rates specified for each item listed below:

1. Instruction one fourth, one fifth, and one eighth grade student

   Instruction, supplies, equipment, and facilities of equal character with those furnished for its own pupils in the public school, in consideration of the sum of $135.00 or actual maintenance cost per pupil unit in average daily attendance.

2. Transportation

   a. Transportation service to be provided for the elementary school pupils to the public school of the party of the second part for a consideration of $_8.00_ per month.

   b. The route to be traveled by the bus in transporting the children shall be as agreed upon by the two contracting parties from time to time and shall be so as best to accommodate the children to be transported, except, however, that the road to be traveled by the bus shall not be laid out over any other than graveled or oiled roads and that during the time that there is snow on the ground the route shall be only over roads which are kept clear of snow.

The first payment for one-half of the school year shall be made by the party of the first part to the party of the second part on or before __January 21__, 19_50_, and the second payment on or before ___June 10___, 19_50_.

It is further agreed by the party of the second part that the teacher or principal of said school shall keep attendance, classification, and scholarship records of all elementary school pupils mentioned herein, and shall make a separate term report for these pupils to the county superintendent for the party of the first part.

It is further agreed between the parties that nothing in this contract shall affect the relationship of these districts as to organization, legal status, and right to receive public money, such as state apportionment, income tax, and special state aid.

IN WITNESS WHEREOF, we have hereunto subscribed our names this day of _August 30_, 19_49_.

School District No. _219J_

Pennington County, Minn.

Ray Rausch Chairman.

Mrs. Alfred Sohm Clerk

School District No. 18

Pennington County, Minn.

O L Wall Chairman.

L W Burns Clerk

Closed School Contract for Instruction with School District 18

During this period, students from School District No. 72-219J did not think of themselves as being County Line students. Most of them, in fact, had no idea that they were. Nine had never gone to school there at all. They were Robert Rausch, Kathryn Solem, Loris Reierson, Gary Hoglin, Judy Reierson, Gerald Rodenbo, Elaine Rodenbo, Donald Rondorf, and Kermit Solem.

In 1954 the school district decided to sell the schoolhouse, and it was put up for sealed bids. LeRoy Reierson submitted the highest bid at three hundred and one dollars,[107] and he moved the building two and one-half miles onto the Reierson farm, where it has served a variety of functions. Without a schoolhouse and with all of its students being transported to school in Thief River Falls, residents of the County Line District waited for a chance to be dissolved and consolidated. By this time, most of the surrounding country schools were also waiting.

The District Finally Ends

A large consolidation ultimately took place. During the summer and fall of 1955, School District No.18 finalized a plan. The first phase called for the Pennington and Marshall County Boards to dissolve up to twenty-five area school districts, including County Line, and then annex them to School District No. 18. Although it was just a formality, it was also necessary for the school board from District No.18 to vote to approve the annexation. The second phase called for the voters of the newly enlarged district to pass a one million two hundred thousand dollar school bond referendum to provide facilities for the expansion.[108] There were two parts to the proposal, and they needed to be voted on separately. The first part asked for one million one hundred and ninety thousand dollars to finance three large building projects. The projects included an addition to the south side of Lincoln High School, a new vocational school on the southeast side of Lincoln, and a new Washington Elementary School. A second part asked for ten thousand dollars for the purchase of a site on the east side of Thief River Falls to build a new grade school at some future date (Mark Twain Elementary and Franklin Middle School were later built on the thirty-four acre site that was purchased for ten thousand dollars on November 27, 1956).[109]

Everything went as planned. School District No. 219J was dissolved by the Pennington County Board of County Commissioners on November 8, 1955, along with seventeen other Pennington County districts. By the time School District No.18 voted to accept the annexations on November 14th, three Marshall County schools had been added as well. The following account appeared on the front page of the Thief River Falls Times on November 16th:

> Following approval last week by the Pennington and Marshall county boards of the dissolution of more than twenty rural school districts tributary to Thief River Falls in the two counties, the board of education of School District

No. 18 voted Monday evening to approve the applications of all the districts for annexation to School District No. 18.

Districts to be attached to the Thief River Falls district include Districts 2, 4, 11, 26, 28, 29, 30, 31, 35, 41, 42, 51, 53, 135, 149, 194, and portions of Districts 125 and 219J in Pennington County; and Districts 118, 133, and 159 in Marshall County.[110]

School District No. 72, the Marshall County portion of County Line School District, was dissolved by the Marshall County Board of County Commissioners on November 18th and annexed to School District No. 18.[111] Three more Pennington County districts were approved for annexation at the following school board meeting: Districts 7, 55, and 127.[112] With the addition of these three districts, phase one of the plan was complete. In all, twenty-four districts had joined with the Thief River District. More would join later.

Despite near blizzard conditions, twelve hundred and ninety-three voters turned out on November 28th to vote on the school bond referendum. Both parts of the proposal were passed by large margins. The first part passed 1080 to 211, while the second part passed 850 to 409.[113] Residents of dissolved School District No. 72-219J were eligible to vote in the election, and many of them did. They were now part of a new district.

The Thief River Falls Teacher Training Program was closed at the end of the 1955-56 school year.[114] The program, which had trained most of the country school teachers who taught in the area, was discontinued by the Pennington County Board due to the small number of remaining rural schools.

The Era of Country Schools in Minnesota Comes to an End

Everywhere in the state, similar scenarios played out as country schools were rapidly being dissolved and annexed to urban districts. By the end of the 1956-57 school year, the number of school districts in Minnesota had been lowered to fewer than thirty-six hundred.[115] The reduced figure led to a statewide renumbering effort in which the state reorganized its educational system into Independent School Districts. On July 1, 1957, Joint Independent Consolidated District No.18 of Pennington and Marshall Counties (Thief River Falls School District) became Independent School District No. 563. One year later, it became Independent School District No. 564, as it is today.

Aimed at dissolving "most of the remaining 'closed' school districts," the 1963 legislature enacted its first mandatory

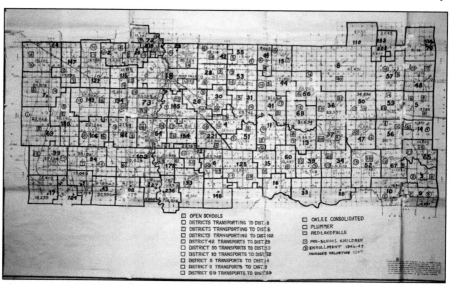

Pennington County School District Map, 1946-47

reorganization legislation. With few exceptions, the legislation automatically dissolved any "closed" district that hadn't joined a district with a high school by July 1, 1965.[116]

Aimed at dissolving the remaining one-room country schools, an even stronger bill was passed in 1967. It mandated that all school districts have both an elementary and a secondary school by 1971.[117] As a result of this legislation, all but three of the state's school districts had a full elementary and secondary program by the end of the 1970-71 school year.[118]

The state department's website listed three hundred and twenty-seven public operating independent school districts in Minnesota as of January 1, 2020. Marshall County had four: Grygla Public School District, located in Grygla; Marshall County Central Schools, located in Newfolden; Stephen-Argyle Central Schools, located in Stephen and Argyle; and Warren-Alvarado-Oslo School District, located in Warren. Pennington County had only two school districts: Thief River Falls School District, located in Thief River Falls; and the Goodridge Public School District, located in Goodridge.

10

Final Thoughts

The names have been permanently etched into my memory: Swanson… Jacobson… Muzzy… Kellberg… Copp… Rausch… Rude… Jensen… Jaennette… Solem. They are among the family names of those who once made up the neighborhood in which I was raised and whose children attended County Line School, in some cases, for more than one generation.

The families lived as a community. Besides going to school together, they also worshiped together, joined clubs and attended meetings together, participated in different types of recreation together, and celebrated special occasions together. During the early nineteen hundreds, County Line was the site of much of this activity, and it served as their cultural center.

The students at County Line School were mainly children and grandchildren of Western European immigrants who came to America looking for a better life. Their families lived on family farms where they worked together developing the land, growing crops, and raising livestock. They were hardy, hardworking, cooperative, and resourceful; essential attributes to bring to a school that was isolated, primitive, and lacking in curriculum.

The majority of the school's teachers were young girls from the area who had backgrounds resembling the students. They typically boarded on neighboring farms and arrived early at the school to start the fires and prepare for the students. As teachers, they had few resources to work with, lacked formal training, and often weren't much older than those they taught. Under difficult circumstances, they did an exceptional job.

Similar to their lives on the farms, everyone at the school contributed to its success. Each student was responsible for a daily chore such as lining up the overshoes, filling the coal bucket, cleaning the chalk erasers, washing the blackboards, hauling in chunks of wood, and so forth. The older students took on additional responsibilities, including tutoring and monitoring those who were waiting for their class time. They all pitched in to prepare the schoolhouse for special events and to clean up the school yard at the end of the year. Everyone was needed and made to feel essential.

Across America as many as two hundred thousand country schools shared similar experiences. Not all of the experiences were pleasant. Some students felt slighted because their school's curriculum offered only the basics, while others felt hampered by a lack of extracurricular activities in areas such as music and athletics. Most, if not all, rural students endured episodes of inclement weather.

The neighborhoods surrounding the schools weren't exempt from unpleasantness either. Efforts to form "breakaway schools" often scarred personal relationships and divided close-knit neighborhoods. The scars took years and sometimes decades to fade away.

Before the early 1900s, the daily lives of rural students rarely extended beyond the walking distance of their homes. The introduction of automobiles, however, revolutionized the way people traveled and greatly expanded the world in which they lived. Autos started to appear in the Thief River Falls community between 1910 and 1915. By the 1930s, most families owned at least one. As the number of autos increased, more attention was given to improving the roads on which they traveled.

The road past County Line School was never improved and during much of the year was impassable by car. Consequently, a large number of the neighborhood events that were once held at the school gradually shifted to Thief River Falls or to Steiner, both of which had superior roads. Most County Line residents chose the Steiner events, even if they had to drive farther. Steiner was small, and the occasions more closely resembled those to which they had become accustomed.

The Steiner School was originally called Excel School, after the township in which it was located. When the Great Northern Railway laid a track by the school in 1904, its location grew into a small town called Steiner, and the school's name changed from Excel to Steiner. Besides the school, the town had a depot, a grain elevator, a stockyard, and a general store. The store, in particular, became an additional attraction for holding community events at Steiner.

Before motorized school buses became available, many rural children were unable to continue their education beyond the eighth grade. High schools were generally located in towns and were too far away for walking. If a rural student wished to attend a high school, it was often necessary to move to a closer site. And because boys were frequently expected to help with the farming, moving wasn't always an option for them.

My parents' experiences were similar to those of many rural students. Dad had been a student at County Line and Mom at the nearby Riverside School. After the eighth grade, my dad stayed home and farmed. He never went to a high school. Mom, meanwhile, continued her education at Lincoln High School in Thief River Falls.

In order to attend Lincoln, it was necessary for Mom to find a home to stay at that was closer to the school. She found a place with a farm family on the outskirts of Thief River Falls, about two miles from the high school. To pay for her room and board, she helped milk the cows before she walked to school in the morning and again after school in the evening.

It would be interesting to learn more about the later lives of County Line students. Where did they live? What further education did they receive? What careers did they pursue? How did they adjust to a different lifestyle beyond the neighborhood?

During my lifetime, I have either met or heard about a large number of County Line students. When my parents were alive, many former students would periodically stop by our farm for visits. The visits gave everyone an opportunity to "catch up" with each other's lives and share what they knew about their classmates.

I recall that most of them had left our area to search for jobs. Because jobs were more plentiful in large cities, many had settled in the Minneapolis-St. Paul area, the closest metropolitan area. I was surprised to learn, though, how far away others had scattered.

The vast majority seem to have led productive and beneficial lives. Several, in fact, are remembered for having made profound contributions in their chosen fields of work. They were exemplary citizens. Many served in the military, and most played active roles in helping improve their communities. I have found no evidence of any student ever being in serious legal trouble or serving time in a prison.

I am convinced that much of the success can be traced back to their roots: the way they were raised at home, and the way they were taught at school. Their ability to work independently as well as in a group, their ability to find ways for overcoming problems, and their persistence in following a task to its completion are all skills that were developed by the time they left school. And because their childhood homes were also their workplaces, a strong work ethic was instilled in them from the day they were born.

Over the years, I have filled out a lot of questionnaires in which the question has been asked, "How long have you worked at your present place of employment?" Being a family farmer myself, I have always replied, "Since birth!" The question seems awkward and inappropriate to me. We do not view what we do as a profession. We see it as a way of life that begins when we are born.

After having a long and noteworthy history, country schools came to an abrupt end. By the middle of the twentieth century, they had become impractical and obsolete. Dependable school buses and improved roads were now available for transporting rural students to large urban schools. The urban schools were far more cost effective and offered increased educational opportunities for the students. By the end of the 1960s, country schools were almost nonexistent.

It will soon be three quarters of a century since the County Line School closed. Needless to say, the neighborhood has drastically changed. Only a few of the old names remain, and among those, there is little communication.

I recently ran into a member of an old family while filling on gas in town. It had been a long time since we had seen each other, and I greeted him by explaining, "I need to go to town to see my neighbors nowadays!" We laughed because it sounded humorous, but I also believe we knew it was true. We miss what has been lost but are unwilling to give up what has been gained.

Rural neighborhoods are no longer close-knit. Without the schools, there is little to hold them together. Technological advances have led us in an ever-expanding world that now stretches far beyond the neighborhood. Our current friends are as likely to live a thousand miles away as to be within walking distance of our homes.

It is useless to blame technology for the changes one doesn't like. Technology is without a conscience and doesn't respond to emotion. I believe that it is beneficial, though, to reflect on the role that country schools played in shaping our nation's history and to acknowledge both their contributions and shortcomings.

I often drive by the County Line site. The one and a half acres of land where the schoolhouse once stood is now part of a large grain field. There are no remnants of the school... yet each time I pass, I can't help but turn my head and glance, as if it was still there.

County Line School lived a full life. It was born at a time when farmers used walking plows and oxen to break the soil. By the time it ended, the world was ready to build rockets to launch humans into outer space. It survived World War I, the Great

Depression, and World War II. During its lifetime, it educated two generations of students and was the site of numerous events and countless stories.

Everything that is alive was born and will someday die. The crop of wheat that is standing there now will also die. But the Creator made certain that life regenerates itself, and the ripened seeds that will be harvested this fall will produce more wheat fields next year.

Schools are like wheat fields. With schools it is knowledge that is planted and later harvested. And like the seeds of wheat that produce more wheat fields, knowledge is fertile, and its fruit will multiply forever.

County Line School, c. 1908

Teacher with County Line students, c. 1908

On ground L to R: Vivian Copp, Goldie Kellberg, Georgia Muzzy, ?, ?, ?, ?, Clara Jacobson, Helmer Kellberg, Annie Johnson. Center on bench L to R: Alice Solem, Esther Kellberg, ?, Mabel Simonson, Mabel Kellberg. Back standing L to R: Ada Jacobson, ?, ?, Harvey Copp, Teacher Abbie Miller, ?, Lida Muzzy, Otto Solem

Teacher leading exercises, 1913-14 school year

L to R: Teacher Anna Adolphs, Alfred Solem, Mabel Jacobson, Arnie Solem, Goldie Kellberg, Raymond Muzzy, Georgia Muzzy, Vernon Copp, Clara Jacobson, Clarence Williams, Ruth Solem

1913-14 School Year

L to R: Teacher Anna Adolphs, Clarence Williams, Ruth Solem, Arnie Solem, Georgia Muzzy, Alfred Solem, Vernon Copp, Mabel Jacobson, Julius Liden, Clara Jacobson, Raymond Muzzy, Goldie Kellberg

Students playing game during recess, 1913-14 school year

1913-14 School Year
Front L to R: Clarence Williams, Vernon Copp, Raymond Muzzy, Ruth Solem, Clara Jacobson, Georgia Muzzy, Goldie Kellberg. Back L to R: Alfred Solem, Mabel Jacobson, Julius Liden

Harold Williams, Alfred Solem, Bernard Jacobson with birdhouses, c. 1917

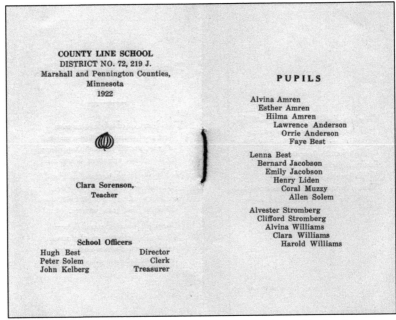

COUNTY LINE SCHOOL
DISTRICT NO. 72, 219 J.
Marshall and Pennington Counties,
Minnesota
1922

Clara Sorenson,
Teacher

School Officers

Hugh Best	Director
Peter Solem	Clerk
John Kelberg	Treasurer

PUPILS

Alvina Amren
Esther Amren
Hilma Amren
Lawrence Anderson
Orrie Anderson
Faye Best

Lenna Best
Bernard Jacobson
Emily Jacobson
Henry Liden
Coral Muzzy
Allen Solem

Alvester Stromberg
Clifford Stromberg
Alvina Williams
Clara Williams
Harold Williams

Souvenir given by teacher to students at close of 1921-22 school year

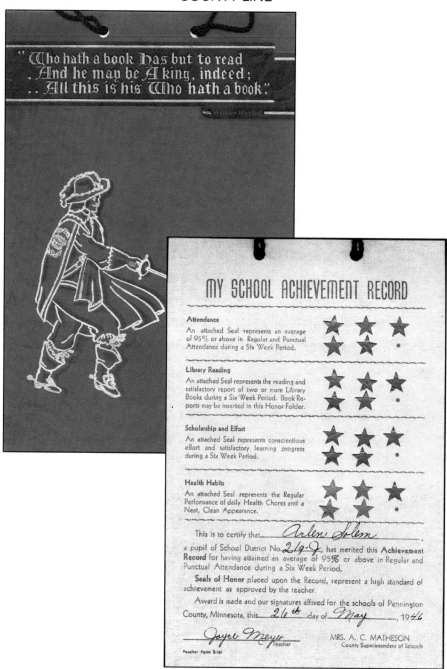

"Who hath a book Has but to read
And he may be A king, indeed;
All this is his Who hath a book".

Wilbur Nesbit

MY SCHOOL ACHIEVEMENT RECORD

Attendance
An attached Seal represents an average of 95% or above in Regular and Punctual Attendance during a Six Week Period.

Library Reading
An attached Seal represents the reading and satisfactory report of two or more Library Books during a Six Week Period. Book Reports may be inserted in this Honor Folder.

Scholarship and Effort
An attached Seal represents conscientious effort and satisfactory learning progress during a Six Week Period.

Health Habits
An attached Seal represents the Regular Performance of daily Health Chores and a Neat, Clean Appearance.

This is to certify that Arlen Solem, a pupil of School District No. 219-9, has merited this Achievement Record for having attained an average of 95% or above in Regular and Punctual Attendance during a Six Week Period.

Seals of Honor placed upon the Record, represent a high standard of achievement as approved by the teacher.

Award is made and our signatures affixed for the schools of Pennington County, Minnesota, this 26th day of May, 1946

Joyce Meyer
Teacher

MRS. A. C. MATHESON
County Superintendent of Schools

Teacher Form 5-181

Presented to Arlen Solem by his teacher, Joyce Meyer, spring of 1946

Bernice Copp, 1943

Lois Copp, 1943

Donna and Janice Rood,
1945-46 school year

First grade students, fall of 1945
Stuart Solem, Janice Rood, Dalys Kellberg,
Philip Jaennette

1940-41 School Year

Front L to R: Dorothy Muzzy, James Rude. Center L to R: James Ayers, Doris Rausch, James Muzzy, Bernice Copp, Helen Rausch, Senora Swanson, Lois Copp. Back L to R: Lawrence Rausch, Lowell Rude, Kenneth Ayers, Herman Rausch, Curtis Swanson, Duane Jensen

Students on nature hike, spring of 1942

Front L to R: Muriel Copp, Lois Copp, Helen Rausch, Dorothy Muzzy, Senora Swanson, Doris Rausch. Back L to R: Rudy Rude, James Rude, James Muzzy, Curtis Swanson, Lowell Rude, Duane Jensen, James Ayers, Herman Rausch, Lawrence Rausch, Kenneth Ayers

Braving the cold, 1943
L to R: Arlen Solem, Muriel Copp, Lowell Rude (seated), Lois Copp, Bernice Copp, Senora Swanson, Dorothy Muzzy, James Rude (seated), James Muzzy

Teacher Joyce Meyer (back) with student teacher Clara Mae Jorde, spring of 1946
Front L to R: Janice Rood, Spencer Johnston, Stuart Solem, Philip Jaennette. Center L to R: James Rude, Donna Rood, Muriel Copp, Dorothy Muzzy, Arlen Solem, Roger Solem

Posing in front of the lone lilac bush in the schoolyard, spring of 1948
L to R: Stuart Solem, James Mattson, Philip Jaennette, Spencer Johnston, Barbara Johnston, Carol Jaennette, Marilyn Mattson

Roger, Arlen, and Stuart Solem, fall of 1948

COUNTY LINE TEACHERS

Clara Mae Jorde
1946-47, 1947-48

Margaret Hanson
1931-32, 1932-33, 1933-34

Bernice Halvorson
1940-41, 1941-42, 1942-43

Adeline Everson
1948-49

Joyce Meyer
1944-45, 1945-46

Enjoying a reunion
Standing: Muriel Copp, Dorothy Muzzy Blodgett, Carol Jaennette Johnson, students. Seated: Joyce Meyer Kron, teacher

Dave Weleski kneeling beside the school stove modified to use in his shop

Judy Reierson Weleski at home with the George Washington portrait from County Line School

APPENDICES

Petitioning

Petitions were used by groups of interested people to either start or end a school district. They were also used by individuals to transfer land, and sometimes district residency, from one district to another. Petitions were heard and acted on by a board of county commissioners who either approved or rejected them at public hearings.

Placed in the appendix, this study on the use of petitions is intended to serve as a resource. While following a sketchy overview of the school's history, it explains the process of petitioning and shows how its usage impacted the history of County Line School. Several of the original documents used in the process are intermittently displayed. In many cases, an account of the formal actions taken at the hearings is also included.

The study is divided into three parts: Petitioning to Start a School District, Petitioning to Transfer Land from One School District to Another, and Petitioning to End a School District.

Petitioning to Start a School District

The first comprehensive legislation to establish and maintain a system of public schools in Minnesota was passed by the state legislature on February 28, 1877,[119] and like most comprehensive acts, its passage was followed by a host of revisions. Included in this lawmaking were several provisions regarding petitioning that the early settlers needed to comply with in order to organize public schools.

Late in 1894, freeholders in Marshall and Polk Counties petitioned their county governments to start a joint school district (land in two counties). According to an 1893 revision, whenever freeholders of one or more school districts desired to organize a new district, they needed to petition the board of county commissioners, and the petition was required to contain the following facts:

- A correct description of the territory to be held in the proposed district.
- The number of persons residing in the proposed district.
- The number of children of school age residing in the proposed district.
- The school districts affected by the organization of the proposed district, the number of children of school age residing in each district so affected, and the number of children which such organization would take from such districts, respectively.
- Signatures by a majority of the freeholders residing within the territory of the proposed new district who are entitled to vote at school meetings in their respective districts.[120]

In each affected county, the completed petition was brought to the county auditor's office and a request was simultaneously made for a hearing with the board of county commissioners. Both counties needed to approve the petition, and before that could be accomplished, a spokesperson for the petition needed to appear at two monthly meetings of each county board. At the first monthly meeting, the spokesperson was required to formally request a hearing to be held at a later meeting. If granted, the commissioners were required to set a date. It was typically set for the next month. Each board was also responsible for completing the following actions prior to the hearing:

- Posting one due notice of the time and place of the hearing in a public place in each of the school districts to be affected by the petition.
- Sending due notice of the time and place of the hearing to the clerk of each affected school district at least ten days prior to the hearing.
- Publishing at least once due notice of the hearing in the legal newspaper of each affected county.
- Receiving affidavits indicating that all three of the due notice requirements listed above were met.[121]

Because the proposal involved a joint district, it was necessary to publish due notice of the hearing in the legal newspaper of both counties, the *Warren Sheaf* in Marshall County and the *Crookston Times* in Polk County. The following notice appeared twice in the *Warren Sheaf* during December of 1894:

> Notice is hereby given that a petition has been filed with the Board of County Commissioners of Marshall County, signed and

acknowledged by a majority of the freeholders who reside in the proposed new district herein described and who are entitled to vote at school meetings in their respective districts, praying for the organization of a new school district out of the territory hereinafter described, and setting forth, substantially, the following facts, to-wit:

FIRST - That the correct description of the territory desired to be embraced in the proposed new district is as follows. viz..

S ½ se ¼ and s ½ sw ¼ sec 31 twp 155 rng 43, s ½ se ¼ and se ¼ sw ¼ sec 36 twp 155 rng 44, sw ¼ sec 5 twp 154 rng 43, e ½ and e ½ w ½ sec 1 twp 154 rng 44, all sec 6 twp 154 rng 43, e ½ ne ¼ sec 24 twp 154 rng 44, all sec 7 twp 154 rng 43, e ½ and e ½ nw ¼ and e ½ sw ¼ sec 12 twp 154 rng 44, all sec 8 twp 154 rng 43, e ½ and e ½ nw ¼ and ne ¼ sw ¼ sec 13 twp 154 rng 44, all sec 17 twp 154 rng 43, all sec 18 twp 154 rng 43, n ½ sec 19 twp 154 rng 43, in the townships of New Solum, Norden, North, and Excel, in said Marshall and Polk Counties, state of Minnesota.

SECOND - That the number of persons residing in the above described territory is 15.

THIRD - That the number of children of school age residing in the above described territory is 24.

FOURTH - That the school districts affected by the organization of the said proposed new district are School District No. 107 of Polk Co., and that the number of children of school age residing therein is 135, and that the number of children of school age which the organization of said proposed new school district would take there-from is none; School District No. 135 of Polk Co., and that the number of children of school age residing therein is 46, and that the number of children of school age which the organization of said proposed new district would take there-from is 4; and School District No. 17 of Marshall Co., and that the number of children of school age residing therein is 63, and that the number of children of school age which the organization of said proposed new school district would take there-from is 11.

Now, therefore, it is hereby ordered and notice is hereby given, that a hearing upon the said petition will be had at a meeting of said board commencing on the 4th day of January A.D. 1895, at 9 o'clock in the forenoon of said day at the County Auditor's office in Warren in said county at which time and place, the said board of county commissioners will hear arguments of all persons interested for, or against, the proposed organization of said new school district.

It is further ordered that a copy of this order and notice be posted in one public place in each of said districts so affected thereby, and a copy thereof served on the clerk of each of said districts so affected at least ten days prior to said time herein set for hearing said petition; and that this order be forthwith once published in the newspaper known as *WARREN SHEAF* which is printed and published in said county and is hereby designated as the legal newspaper for publishing the same.

Dated this 19th day of December A. D. 1894.

By order of the Board of County Commissioners of Marshall County, Minnesota.

By D. B. Bakke, Chairman of said Board.[122]

Two additional requirements had to be met before the petition could be approved. First, the petition was to be read during the hearing, and all interested persons, for and against, were to be given an opportunity to be heard and considered. Second, the county superintendent's signature of approval was necessary on the petition. Because superintendents were entrusted with the well-being of county schools, they were obligated to only sign petitions that, if approved, were unlikely to cause undue harm to existing schools.

Hearings were held in both counties. The Marshall County Board of County Commissioners held its hearing on January 4, 1895, in Warren. The Polk County Board of County Commissioners held theirs on January 8th in Crookston. At both hearings, the petition was approved and a new school district, 72-219J (County Line), was ordered.

> Petition for the formation of a new school district made by Edward E. Engen and others, granted and it was ordered that the following described territory be formed into School District No. to-wit:
>
> S ½ se ¼ and s ½ sw ¼ sec 31 twp 155 rng 43, sw ¼ sec 5 twp 154 rng 43, all sec 6 twp 154 rng 43, all sec 7 twp 154 rng 43, all sec 8 twp 154 rng 43, all sec 17 twp 154 rng 43, all sec 18 twp 154 rng 43, n ½ sec 19 twp 154 rng 43, e ½ and e ½ w ½ sec 1 twp 154 rng 44, e ½ ne ¼ sec 24 twp 154 rng 44, e ½ and e ½ nw ¼ and e ½ of sw ¼ sec 12 twp 154 rng 44, e ½ and e ½ nw ¼ and ne ¼ sw ¼ sec 13 twp 154 rng 44, s ½ se ¼ and se ¼ sw ¼ sec 36 twp 155 rng 44.[123]

Eight years later, on April 9, 1903, a small group of freeholders mainly from the County Line District drafted a controversial petition to start a "breakaway district." A signed petition was brought to the auditors of Red Lake and Marshall Counties, and hearings were requested. At both ensuing board meetings, public hearings were granted, and orders were issued to ensure that the affected school districts receive proper notice.

Petition for the Formation of a New School District, side 1

STATE OF MINNESOTA,
County of *Red Lake* } ss.   BE IT KNOWN, That on this *9th* day of
April, 1903, before me personally appeared
Olaf Flieen Jr. Haldor Erickson, Ben Anderson
John S. Smith, Siver Knudsen Aug. Soderberg
E. E. Erickson, Aud Dux Johanne F. Finke
Mrs. Mathilda Smith

to me personally known to be the signers of the above petition, and freeholders who are entitled to vote at
school meetings in their respective districts, residing within the territory in the foregoing petition described
and proposed to be organized into a new School District, and each acknowledged that *they* signed and
executed the said petition as *their* free act and deed.
                                                          John L. Finke
                                                          Justice of the Peace

STATE OF MINNESOTA,
County of *Red Lake* } ss.
John L. Finke being by me first duly sworn, doth depose and
say that he is a resident of the territory described in the within petition, and knows all the freeholders who
are legal voters residing in the said territory to be affected by the within petition, and that the within petition
is signed by a majority of the freeholders who are legal voters residing in the territory to be affected by the
within petition.
                                                          John L. Finke

Subscribed and sworn to before me, this *10th* day of *April* A.D. 1903
                                                          Frak Richardson
                                                          Notary Public
                                                          for Red Lake Co.,
                                                          Minn.

STATE OF MINNESOTA,
County of *Red Lake* } ss.
I HEREBY CERTIFY, That, in my opinion, it is proper that the prayer of the within petition should be
granted, and I hereby recommend that the same be granted.
                                                          Frank Jeffers
                                                          County Superintendent of Schools.

PETITION FOR FORMATION OF NEW SCHOOL DISTRICT.

Filed the *11th* day of *April* 1903

James C. _____
County Auditor

Petition for the Formation of a New School District, side 2

The orders, which had been signed by the auditor and board chair of each county, listed the three due notice requirements that needed to be followed.

Order for Hearing on School District Petition for Formation of New District

The notice requirements had been modified since the formation of County Line in 1895. A 1901 amendment mandated that the notice be "published at least twice in the legal newspaper"[124] of each affected county and "served by the county auditor by mail"[125] to the clerk of each affected school district. It further ordered that all three, not just the posting requirement, be executed "at least ten days before the time of such hearing."[126] As before it was the responsibility of each affected county board to make sure that the notice requirements were met and verified prior to a hearing.

The proposed district was located entirely in Red Lake County. It included portions of three school districts: County Line, Willowdale (District No. 2), and City View (District No. 135). One of the petitioners, Olaf Thoen, Jr., posted a notice on each of the schoolhouse doors and later signed an affidavit before Justice of the Peace John Finke for legal verification.

The county auditor mailed notices to the clerk of each affected school district: Peter O. Solem of County Line, J. G. Nordhagen of Willowdale, and L. J. Parbst of City View. He also sent notices to be published twice in both legal newspapers, *The St. Hilaire Spectator* in Red Lake County and *The Warren Sheaf* in Marshall County.

Both county boards held July hearings on the petition with different results. Red Lake County approved the petition on the fourteenth, while Marshall County rejected it on the fifteenth. A refusal by the Marshall County Superintendent of Schools to sign the petition was the apparent reason for rejection.

No. 1074.—Notice of Hearing on Petition to Form New School District, with Affidavits of Service. Laws of 1891-1892-1901. Class 2.

SCHOOL DISTRICT NOTICE.

Notice is Hereby Given *That a petition has been filed with the Board of County Commissioners of* Red Lake *County, signed and acknowledged by a majority of the freeholders who reside in the proposed new district herein described, and who are entitled to vote at school meetings in their respective districts, praying for the organization of a new school district out of the territory hereinafter described, and setting forth, substantially, the following facts, to-wit:*

FIRST—That the correct description of the territory desired to be embraced in the proposed new district is as follows, viz: The South-east quarter and the east one half of the south-west quarter of Section Twelve (12), all of Section thirteen (13), The east one half of section fourteen (14), the north-east quarter and the north one half of the south-east quarter of Section twenty-three (23), the north one half, and the north one half of the south-west quarter and the north one half of the south-east quarter of Section twenty-four (24) all in Township one Hundred and fifty-four (154), Range forty-four (44).

Also, the west one half of the South-west quarter of Section seven (7), the west one half and the south-east quarter of section eighteen (18) and all of section nineteen (19), all in township one hundred and fifty-four (154), Range Forty-three (43)

in the Townships of Norden and North *in said* Red Lake *County, State of Minnesota.*

SECOND—That the number of persons residing in the above described territory is ~~Fifteen (15)~~ *Seventy-five*

THIRD—That the number of children of school age residing in the above described territory is Thirty-six (36)

FOURTH—That the school districts affected by the organization of the said proposed new district are School District No. 219 *and that the number of children of school age residing therein is* Thirty-six (36) *and that the number of children of school age which the organization of said proposed new school district would take therefrom is* Fifteen (15) *also School District No.* 135 *and that the number of children of school age residing therein is* Thirty-eight (38) *and that the number of children of school age which the organization of said proposed new district would take therefrom is* Four (4) *also School District No.* 2 *and that the number of children of school age residing therein is* Forty (40) *and that the number of children of school age which the organization of said proposed new school district would take therefrom is* Nine (9)

FIFTH—That the said proposed new district does not include the school building of any existing school district.

Now, Therefore, *It is hereby ordered, and notice is hereby given, that a hearing upon the said petition will be had at a meeting of said Board, commencing on the* Fourteenth *day of* July *A. D. 190* 3, *at* one *o'clock in the* after *noon of said day, at* the Office of the County Auditor in the City of Red Lake Falls *in said County, at which time and place the said Board of County Commissioners will hear arguments of all persons interested for or against the proposed organization of said new school district.*

It is Further Ordered, *That a notice of said hearing be posted in one public place in each of said districts so affected thereby, and a copy thereof served on the Clerk of each of said districts so affected at least ten days prior to said time herein set for hearing said petition; and that said notice be forthwith twice published in the newspaper known as* The St. Hilaire Spectator *which is printed and published in said County and is hereby designated as the legal newspaper for publishing the same.*

Dated this twenty-third *day of* May *A. D. 190* 3.

By order of the Board of County Commissioners of Red Lake *County, Minnesota.*

By James Sutor

Chairman of said Board.

Notice of Hearing on Petition to Form New School District, with Affidavits of Service, side 1

State of Minnesota, } ss.
County of _Red Lake_

Olaf Thoen Jr being first duly sworn, says that he posted copies of the within notice in one public place of each of said school districts, as follows, to-wit: One copy thereof on the front door of the school house in School District No. _2_ of said County, on the _22 nd_ day of _June_ 1903, one copy thereof on the front door of the school house in School District No. _133_ in said County, on the _22 nd_ day of _June_ 1903 one copy thereof on the front door of the school house in School District No. _219_ in said County, on the _22 nd_ day of _June_ 1903

SUBSCRIBED AND SWORN TO BEFORE ME, this _27th_ day of _June_ 1903.

John I. Fjelde
Justice of the Peace

Olaf Thoen Jr.

State of Minnesota, } ss.
County of _Red Lake_

I, _James E. Good_ County Auditor of _Red Lake_ County, Minnesota, do hereby certify that I served a copy of the within notice upon _J. G. Nordhagen_ Clerk of School District No. _2_, and one copy upon _L. J. Parbst_ Clerk of School District No. _132_, and one copy upon _Pete Solem_ Clerk of School District No. _219_, by depositing the said copy in the postoffice at _Red Lake Falls_ Minnesota, addressed to each of said above named Clerks at their respective places of postoffice address, (residence,) postage prepaid, on the _16th_ day of _June_ 1903

Witness, My hand and seal of office at _Red Lake Falls_ Minnesota, this _16th_ day of _June_ A. D. 1903

James E. Good
County Auditor of _Red Lake_ County, Minnesota.

Notice of Hearing on Petition to Form New School District, with Affidavits of Service, side 2

Because County Line was a joint district, the petition needed to be approved by both counties. Consequently, petitioners submitted a second petition to the Marshall County Board later in the year. It was basically the same as the first except with more signatures.

The second petition took longer to resolve. According to the board's minutes, it was tabled twice; once on November 27, 1903, and again on January 7, 1904.

> "The petition of Johanna Finke and others for the formation of a new school district of part of joint School District No. 72 of Marshall County and No. 219 in Red Lake County, laid on the table."[127]

> "On motion resolved, that the petition of Johanna Finke and others for the formation of a new school district of part of joint School District No. 72 in Marshall County and No. 219 in Red Lake County be laid on the table. Resolution carried."[128]

There is nothing more in the minutes to indicate what further action was taken. It is written on the document itself, however, that it was rejected. Immediately below the rejection notice is the signature of the board's chairman along with the date, which is given as January 7, 1904. No explanation was offered for the rejection. However, just as with the first petition, it was never signed by the Marshall County Superintendent of Schools.

Despite the two rejections by the Marshall County Board, a new school district, District No. 25, was eventually organized. According to Red Lake County tax records, the new district began receiving its operating revenue in the fall of 1905.[129] Exactly how and when it was finally organized, though, is unclear as there is no indication that the Marshall County petition was ever signed by the Marshall County Superintendent.

Petitioning to Transfer Land from One School District to Another

Hearings on petitions by individuals wanting to transfer land from one school district to another were quite common. However, the number of hearings that affected any given district was generally low. The County Line District, for an example, had fewer than a dozen transfer requests during its sixty-one years of existence.

Transfer petitions were used for a variety of reasons. Most frequently, though, they were used by landowners who either wanted lower tax rates on the land involved, shorter and less obstructive routes to school for their children, or preferred schools with which to be associated. Sometimes more than one objective was involved.

The successful petitions usually focused on the students' route to school and either dealt with the travel distance or certain natural barriers along the way. County boards made sure that the students' safety and comfort were of primary concern. Petitions that focused on other issues were usually given less consideration.

When new districts were established, there often were landowners who preferred to remain in their former district. This was the case with Peter O. Solem, who petitioned to transfer back into the Steiner District shortly after the County Line District was organized. Solem had developed a close relationship with the Steiner community and wanted the connection to continue. His request was rejected by the Marshall County Board:

> "Petition of Peter Solem to be set off from joint School District No. 219 Polk Co. and 72 Marshall Co. to District No. 17, rejected."[130]

The most common reason for requesting a transfer was to shorten the travel distance to school. Winter weather in Northwest Minnesota was harsh, and bitterly cold temperatures were often a worry. Extended exposure to the cold could easily result in severe frostbite or possibly even death.

The first successful petition affecting County Line was accomplished by R.L. Muzzy in the fall of 1903, shortly after the County Line District had moved its schoolhouse to the prairie location. His school-age children had been attending Steiner School in District No. 17, but because the County Line schoolhouse was now located closer to the Muzzy home than the Steiner schoolhouse, he wanted to send them to County Line.

To achieve this goal, Muzzy needed to submit a transfer petition to each affected county, Marshall and Red Lake, and the commissioners from each county needed to approve the petition at a public hearing. During the process, both Muzzy and the commissioners were required to follow certain legal requirements. Below is a list of the requirements that existed at the time:

- The petitioner needed to be a legal voter, freeholder, and resident of the school district to be set off.

- The lands described in the petition needed to adjoin the school district to be attached to.
- The petition needed to list the reason(s) for transferring land from one school district to another.
- In each affected county, the petitioner was required to make a formal request for a hearing of the petition at a county board of commissioners meeting.
- In each affected school district, due notice of the time and place of the hearing needed to be posted in one public place at least ten days prior to the hearing.
- In each affected school district, due notice of the time and place of the hearing needed to be hand delivered and left with the clerk at least ten days prior to the hearing.
- In each affected county, signed affidavits indicating that the two due notice requirements listed above had been met needed to be received by the county board of commissioners prior to the hearing.
- In each affected county, the petition was to be read during the hearing and all interested persons, for and against, were to be given the opportunity to be heard and considered.
- In each affected county, a written approval of the petition was required by the County Superintendent of Schools.

Muzzy's petition was a request to transfer land, including his place of residence, from the Steiner District to the County Line District. The reason given was "that from the southwest corner of the above-described land, it is one mile to the schoolhouse in District # 72; whereas, the distance from the above described land to the schoolhouse in District # 17 is two and one half miles."[131] The petition was granted on September 25, 1903 by the Marshall County Board of Commissioners.

Petition by Legal Voter to be Set Off, side 1

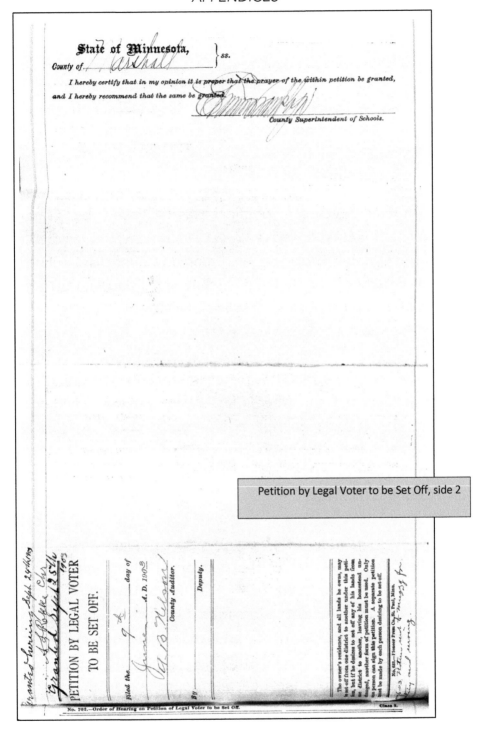

State of Minnesota,

County of......Marshall...... } ss.

I hereby certify that in my opinion it is proper that the prayer of the within petition be granted, and I hereby recommend that the same be granted.

County Superintendent of Schools.

Petition by Legal Voter to be Set Off, side 2

PETITION BY LEGAL VOTER
TO BE SET OFF.

Filed the 7th day of
June A. D. 190 3
County Auditor.
By Deputy.

The owner's residence, and all lands he owns, may be set off from one district to another under this petition, but if he desires to set off any of his lands from one district to another, leaving his homestead unchanged, another form of petition must be used. Only the person can sign this petition. A separate petition must be made by each person desiring to be set off.

No. 702.—Order of Hearing on Petition of Legal Voter to be Set Off.

Class R.

"On motion resolved, that the petition of R.L. Muzzy to have his land, the nw ¼ of Section 9 in Township 154, Range 43, set off from School District No. 17 and attached to School District No. 72, be granted. Resolution carried."[132]

Another successful petition was achieved by Clara Jaennette in 1946. Widowed in 1934, Clara's oldest two children, James and Dorothy Muzzy, began attending County Line during the 1938-39 school year. At the time, they were living with Clara's parents in Section 9 of North Township and in the County Line District. After remarrying she moved to a new location in Section 5 of Excel Township, about a mile farther north. The new location was in the Steiner District, but the children continued going to school at County Line. When Clara's youngest two children, Philip and Carol Jaennette, approached school age, she petitioned to transfer the north farm into the County Line District. The petition was granted, and all four of her children graduated from County Line School.

"At 11:00 a.m. on January 9, 1946 a hearing was had on the matter of the petition of Mrs. Clara Jaennette to have the SE ¼ of Section 5, Township 154, Range 43 set aside from Marshall County School District No. 17 and annexed to Pennington-Marshall Joint School District No. 72-219. No one appeared before the Board in opposition to the petition and the County Board of Marshall County having approved the request contained in said petition at its meeting held on August 7, 1945, it was moved by Mabey and seconded by Hyland that the request contained in the petition of Mrs. Clara Jaennette be approved."[133]

Lester Halvorson owned a farm along the southeast border of the County Line School District. Although he lived in School District No. 18 (Thief River Falls) and his son Lloyd attended Thief River Falls schools, much of his farmland was located in the County Line District. Consequently, Halvorson paid property taxes that went to support both school districts. Prior to 1947, Minnesota landowners in school districts without a high school didn't have to pay for the tuition of students from their district who attended high schools outside of their district. That tax incentive was eliminated during the 1947 legislative session, resulting in a substantial property tax increase for Halvorson's "County Line land." On July 10, 1950, Halvorson petitioned the Pennington County Board to transfer his "County Line land" into the Thief River Falls District. The petition was denied.

> "It was moved by Tasa and seconded by Hanson that the petition of Lester N. Halvorson to have Lots 1, 2, and 3 and NW ¼ SW ¼, W ½ NW ¼, E ½ NW ¼ all in Sec. 16-154-43 detached from Joint School District No. 219-72 and attached to School District No. 18 be and the same is hereby denied."[134]

State of Minnesota, }

County of..........PENNINGTON

LESTER N. HALVORSON

SCHL DIST NO. 219-72 to 18

Notice of Hearing on Petition for School District Set-off

Notice is Hereby Given, *That*..........LESTER N. HALVORSON..........

has filed his petition with the County Board of said County stating he is a freeholder and resident in said County; that he owns land now in School District No...........219-72..........*in said County described as follows, to-wit:* Lots 1, 2 and 3 (Less Ry) and NW¼SW¼,

W½NW¼ (Less Ry), E½NW¼, all in Section 16, Twp 154, Rge 43.

which land Adjoins.......... *School District*

..........("adjoins" or "is separated from")..........

No. 18 *in said County*..........

..........(describe intervening land, if any; and state it is vacant and unoccupied or that owner is unknown)..........

and petitioning, for reasons therein stated, that his said land..........

..........(and said intervening land, if any)..........

be set off from said School District No. 219-72 *to said School District No.* 18 *;*

AND THAT SAID PETITION WILL BE HEARD at a regular *meeting*

of said Board on the 8th *day of* August 19 50*, at*

2:30 *o'clock* P. M. *at* Commissioners room in Court house

in the City *of* Thief River Falls *in said County.*

Dated July 22nd *, 19* 50*.*

By Order of the County Board:

..........County Auditor.

Notice of Hearing on Petition for School District Set-off

Petitioning to End a School District

Petitioning was also used to end a school district. The process of ending a district involved two basic steps: dissolving one district and then annexing it to another. To accomplish the task, both districts needed to be in agreement. A school district could not be dissolved unless another district was willing to accept it.

During the 1950-51 school year, the residents of County Line School District decided to end their district. Below is a list of legal requirements that needed to be followed:

- The petition needed to be signed by ninety percent of the freeholders qualified to vote at school meetings of their district.
- The petition needed to list the reason(s) for dissolving the school district.
- In each affected county, the petitioners were required to make a formal request for a hearing of the petition at a county board of commissioners meeting.
- In each affected county, due notice of the time and place of the hearing was required to be published in the legal newspaper for two consecutive weeks prior to the hearing.
- In each affected school district, due notice of the time and place of the hearing needed to be posted in three of the most public places at least ten days prior to the hearing.

- In each affected school district, due notice of the time and place of the hearing needed to be mailed to the clerk at least ten days prior to the hearing.
- In each affected county, signed affidavits indicating that the three due notice requirements listed above had been met needed to be received by the county board of commissioners prior to the hearing.
- In each affected county, the petition was to be read during the hearing and all interested persons, for and against, were to be given an opportunity to be heard and considered.
- In each affected county, a written approval of the petition was required by the County Superintendent of Schools.

On February 27, 1951, the County Line School Board filed a petition at the Pennington County Auditor's office to dissolve School District No. 72-219J and annex it to School District No.18 of

Petition for Change of Boundaries, Consolidation, or Annexation of School Districts, side 1a

Pennington County. Since County Line was a joint school district, the petition was also filed at the Marshall County office. The petition had the required number of freeholder signatures, and

Fifth—That, in case this petition is granted, the number of said children that will be taken from School District No. 219-72JT and transferred to School District No. 18 , is 6

Sixth—That the reasons for the ....(2)

are as follows, to-wit: ....

Wherefore your petitioners pray that ....(3)

as hereinbefore specified.   Respectfully submitted

NAMES OF PETITIONERS	Residing in District No.	NAMES OF PETITIONERS	Residing in District No.
Edwin L. Swanson	72-219J	Clara Jaenette	
Ray Rausch		LeRoy Rierson	
Florence Rausch		Gladys Rierson	
Rebecca Solem	72-219J	Roy Rude	
Alfred Solem		Mabel Rude	
Morris Johnson			
Elida Johnson			
LaVerne L. Rondorf			
Olive Rondorf			
Vernon Copp			
C.C. Jensen			
Anna Jensen			
V.E. Copp			
Mrs. Mike Elgert			

Petition for Change of Boundaries, Consolidation, or Annexation of School Districts, side 1b

State of Minnesota, } ss. (4)
County of Pennington

On this 27th day of February

19 51, *personally came before me*
Edwin L. Swanson, Ray Rausch, and Rebecca Solem, to me known
to be three of the persons who signed the goregoing petition and who
obtained the remaining signatures appearing on the said petition

to me well known to be persons who signed the foregoing petition, and each stated that he had read the petition and knows the contents thereof and acknowledged that he executed the same as his free act and deed.

Gunnuf Gunstenson

My Commission Expires

_____ 19 ____

Notary Public GUNNUF GUNSTENSON, (SEAL)
County, Minnesota Notary Public, PENNINGTON CO., MINN.
My commission expires NOV. 28, 1954.

State of Minnesota, } ss. (5)
County of Marshall-Pennington

I hereby certify that the foregoing petition is signed
by 90 *per cent of the freeholders qualified to vote at school meetings in School District No.* 72-219J
in said County.

Dated February 27 19 51

Mrs. Rebecca Solem

Clerk of School District No. 72-219J

State of Minnesota, } ss. (5)
County of _____

I hereby certify that the foregoing petition is signed
by _____ *per cent of the freeholders qualified to vote at school meetings in School District No.*
in said County.

Dated _____ 19 ____

Clerk of School District No. _____

State of Minnesota, } ss. (5)
County of _____

I hereby certify that the foregoing petition is signed by _____ *per cent of the freeholders qualified*
to vote at school meetings in District No. _____ *in said County.*

Dated _____ 19 ____

Clerk of School District No. _____

State of Minnesota, } ss.
County of Pennington
of Pennington

I, County Superintendent of Schools of the County
State of Minnesota, hereby certify that the foregoing
petition has been submitted to me for approval; and that the same is by me _____ *approved for the follow-*
ing reasons, to-wit:

That there will be only five pupils attending for some time to come
and it will be impossible to operate efficiently

Petition for Change of Boundaries, Consolidation, or
Annexation of School Districts, side 2

Dated Feb. 27 19 51

Mrs. A.G. Matheson

County Superintendent of Schools.

Note (1) If for consolidation, insert "said districts be consolidated into one _____District";
if for annexation, insert "said School District No. _____ be annexed to said School
District No. _____", etc. If for change of boundaries, insert "the boundaries of said
districts be changed as follows, to-wit:" and follow with full description or statement of the
change.

Note (2) Insert "consolidation of said districts," or "annexation of said School District No. _____
to School District No." or "For the change of boundaries of said districts," as the case may be.

Note (3) Insert "said districts be consolidated," or "said School District No. _____ be
annexed to said District No. _____" or "the boundaries of said districts be
changed," as the case may be.

Note (4) If acknowledgments are taken on different dates, or by different persons, or there is not room
enough, attach other certificates in same form.

Note (5) No certificates are provided for by Statute; but there must be some proof that petition is signed
by a certain percentage of freeholders; hence certificates are added.

it listed the reasons for its request. It also had a written approval of the petition by the Pennington County Superintendent of Schools, Martha Matheson.

The three due notice requirements were followed according to law. Notices of the hearings were published twice in both legal newspapers, the *Thief River Falls Times* and the *Warren Sheaf*. Edwin Swanson, treasurer of the County Line District, posted notices in three of the most public places in District No. 72-219J, and the Pennington County Sheriff posted notices in three of the most public places in District No. 18.

State of Minnesota,

County of Marshall } ss. Edwin L. Swanson, being duly sworn,

on oath says: that on the twenty-fourth day of March, 19 51,

he posted true and correct copies of the within notice in a manner likely to attract attention in three of the most public places in School District No. 72 in said County, to-wit: One copy at Northeast corner of the Northwest quarter of section 6, Lot 3 by the gravel pit.

one copy at North side ½ mile west of the northeast corner of the northeast quarter of section 7.

and one copy at Southwest corner of the Northwest quarter of section 9 along highway No. 32.;

and that on the day of, 19, he posted true and correct copies of said notice in manner likely to attract attention in three of the most public places in School District No. in said County, to-wit: One copy thereof at Posting of notice in District 18 will be posted by the sheriff of one copy thereof at Pennington County.

and one copy thereof at

Subscribed and Sworn to before me this 27th

day of March, 19 51

Esther Lane

ESTHER LANE
Deputy County Auditor
Notary Public, County, Minn.

My Commission expires 12-31-54

Edwin L. Swanson

Affidavit for public postings

It is interesting to note that one of the three most public places in the County Line District was located "by the gravel pit."

NOTICE OF HEARING ON PETITION

NOTICE IS HEREBY GIVEN, That whereas a petition has been presented to the County Board of Marshall County, Minnesota, on the 6th day of March 1951, purporting to be signed by 90 per cent of the freeholders qualified to vote at school meeting residing is the school district known as School District No.72 Joint 219 of Marshall and Pennington Counties respectively, praying that said School District 72-Joint 219 be annexed to Independent School District No. 18 of Pennington County, for the following reasons, to wit: That there will be only five pupils attending for some time to come and therefore will be impossible to operate efficiently.

IT IS THEREFORE ORDERED, That said petition be heard at a meeting of said Board to be held at the County Court house in the City of Warren in said County on Tuesday the 3rd day of April 1951, at 11:00 o'clock A. M.,,at which time and place this Board will hear all persons interested, and their evidence and arguments, for and against the granting of said petition.

IT IS FURTHER ORDERED, That notice of said hearing be given by the publication of this order for two consecutive weeks prior to said hearing in the official newspaper and by posting of copies thereof in three of the most public places in each of the above specified districts, and by mailing copies of this order to the clerks of each of said districts, according to law.

THE COUNTY BOARD OF MARSHALL COUNTY, MINNESOTA

Attest:

Levi G. Johnson
County Auditor

By Sofus H. Bjertness
Vice Chairman

Notice of April 3, 1951 Hearing on Petition for Annexation with School District 18

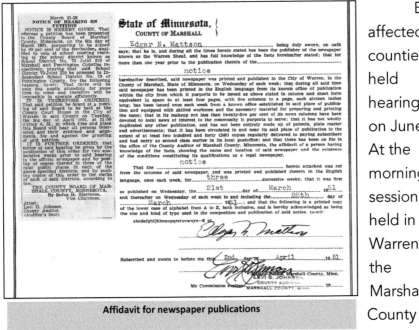

Affidavit of Publication to be Attached

State of Minnesota, }ss.

County of...... Marshall

I, the undersigned, hereby certify: that on the...... Twenty-first ......day of...... March ...... 19 51, I mailed to...... Mrs. Alfred Solem ...... as clerk of School District No. 72-219 Joint ...... in said County at the following address...... Thief River Falls, Rt. 2, Minnesota ...... and to...... Lloyd Bennes ......as clerk of School District No. 18 Pennington/County in said County at the following address...... Thief River Falls, Minnesota ...... true and correct copies of the within notice, by enclosing the same in sealed envelopes and depositing them in the Post Office at...... Warren, Minnesota ...... in said County, postage prepaid.

County Auditor,...... Marshall ......County, Minn.

Affidavit for clerk mailings

Finally, notices were mailed to the clerk of each affected school district: Mrs. Alfred Solem, clerk of District No. 72-219J; and Lloyd Bennes, clerk of District No. 18.

Affidavit for newspaper publications

Both affected counties held hearings on June 5th. At the morning session held in Warren, the Marshall County

Commissioners decided to "postpone action pending the outcome of the hearing in Pennington County."[135] At the afternoon session held in Thief River Falls, the petition to dissolve was denied by the Pennington County Commissioners because an "objection was made to the annexation." School District No. 18 was not yet willing to annex the County Line School District.

Commissioner Olson offered the following resolution and moved its adoption:

WHEREAS, a petition was filed in the Office of the County Auditor of Pennington County on February 26, 1951 by Edwin L. Swanson and other freeholders in Joint School District No. 72-219, praying that Joint School District No. 72-219 be dissolved and annexed to Independent School District No. 18 of Pennington County, and

WHEREAS, said petition was presented to the Pennington County Board at its regular meeting held on March 3, 1951 at which meeting the County Board set a hearing on said petition for 2:00 p.m., April 3, 1951 at which hearing the hearing was continued to 2:00 p.m. June 5, 1951, and

WHEREAS, the final hearing was held on the said petition at the regular meeting of the Pennington County Board at 2:00 p.m., June 5, 1951, and

WHEREAS, at the hearing held at 2:00 p.m., June 5, 1951 representation was had and objection was made to the annexation of Joint School District No. 72-219 to Independent School District No. 18 of Pennington County,

NOW THEREFORE BE IT RESOLVED, that the said petition of Edwin L. Swanson and other freeholders of Joint School District No. 72-219 be and the same is hereby denied.

The foregoing resolution was seconded by Commissioner Hanson and CARRIED.[136]

As a result of the denial, the County Line School District continued transporting its students to other districts until the 1955-56 school year. By then most of the country schools surrounding Thief River Falls were also ready to dissolve, and the Thief River Falls District was ready to annex them.

The effort to dissolve District No. 219J (the Pennington County part of County Line School District) was a joint effort. Eighteen districts from Pennington County, including 219J, submitted petitions which were handled collectively by the Pennington County Board of County Commissioners. The following is a joint notice of the November 8th hearing that appeared in the *Thief River Falls Times*:

WHEREAS, a resolution adopted by the electors of School District No. 2, 4, 11, 26, 28, 29,

30, 31, 35, 41, 42, 51, 53, 125, 135, 149, 194, and 219J of Pennington County, Minnesota, at legal meetings, and properly certified by the Clerks of said Districts, and presented to the County Board of said County on the 4th day of October, 1955 praying for the dissolution of said School Districts and duly approved by the Superintendent of Schools of said County.

IT IS THEREFORE ORDERED, That a hearing be held on said Resolutions at a meeting of said Board at Thief River Falls in the Commissioners' Room of the Courthouse in said County, on Tuesday the 8th day of November, 1955, at 10:00 o' clock a.m., at which time and place this Board will hear all persons interested, and their evidence and arguments for and against dissolving said School Districts.

IT IS FURTHER ORDERED, That notice of said hearing be given by the publication of this order for two consecutive weeks prior to said hearing in the newspaper known as the *Thief River Falls Times*, published and printed in said County; by the posting of copies thereof in three of the most public places in each of the above named school districts affected thereby, at least ten days before said day of hearing; and by the mailing of a copy thereof to the Clerk of each of the above named school districts affected thereby at least ten days before said day of hearing, according to law.

The County Board of Pennington County, Minnesota,
By M. A. Lindberg, Chairman.
Attest. C. W. Rodekuhr, County Auditor[137]

The consolidation plan proceeded smoothly. At the November 8th hearing, the Pennington County Board dissolved seventeen school districts and annexed them to District No.18 with a single vote. One of them was 219J.

Commissioner Olson introduced the following resolution and moved its adoption:
WHEREAS, Pursuant to notice duly given as provided by law and the order of said Board; and the said Board having heard all persons interested in said matter, both for and against, finds as follows;

First — That resolutions adopted by the electors of said school districts at legal meetings and properly certified by the Clerk of said Districts, were presented to said Board on the 4th day of October, 1955, praying for the dissolution of said School Districts and duly approved by Superintendent of Schools of said County.

Second — That notice of a hearing on said resolutions was duly given by publication of the order of said Board for said hearing in the newspaper known as the *Thief River Falls Times*, published and printed in said County, for two consecutive weeks prior to said day of hearing; and by the posting of copies of said order in three of the most public places in each of the school districts affected thereby for at least ten days before said day of hearing; and by service of said order by mail upon each of the Clerks of the school districts affected thereby, at least ten days before said day of hearing.

Third — That it is expedient and will be for the best interests of the residents and children of school age of said common School Districts No. 2, 4, 11, 26, 28, 29, 30, 31, 35, 41, 42, 51, 53, 135, 149, 194, and 219J, to have said districts dissolved and the territory embraced therein attached to other existing school districts, as hereinafter set forth, for the following reasons, to-wit: So that the school districts may mutually operate a larger school to give their children better school facilities at a more economical cost.

NOW THEREFORE IT IS ORDERED, That the said resolutions be, and the same hereby are granted and that School Districts 2, 4, 11, 26, 28, 29, 30, 31, 35, 41, 42, 51, 53, 135, 149, 194, and 219J are hereby attached to Independent Consolidated District No. 18 and become liable for their proportionate share of the Bonded debt of School District No. 18.

The foregoing resolution was duly seconded by Commissioner Anderson and declared carried.[138]

A few minutes later, the board acted on the eighteenth district, No. 125, with a separate resolution. It was dissolved and divided into two parts. One part was annexed to District No. 16 and the other part to District No. 18.

The petition to dissolve District No. 72 (the Marshall County part of County Line School District) was handled differently. Both the notices and the hearing were done individually. On November 18th, ten days after 219J was dissolved by the Pennington County Board of County Commissioners, the Marshall County Board voted to approve the dissolution of District No. 72.

Commissioner Rapacz offered the following resolution and moved its adoption:

WHEREAS, a resolution was adopted by the majority of the electors of Common School District No. 219 of Pennington, joint with No. 72 of Marshall County, at a meeting of said Joint District, praying for the dissolution of said School District, and for having the territory embraced therein attached to Independent School District No. 18 of Pennington County, and

WHEREAS, pursuant to notice a hearing was held on said resolution by the County Board of Pennington County, on November 8th, 1955, at which meeting, It Was Ordered, that said resolution be granted, and that said School District be attached to Independent School District No. 18 of Pennington County.

BE IT RESOLVED, by the Board of County Commissioners of Marshall County, that the action taken by the County Board of Pennington County be, and the same is hereby approved, that said School District No. 219-Joint 72 be dissolved and that the territory comprising the same be attached to and made a part of Independent Consolidated School District No. 18 of Pennington and Marshall Counties.

Commissioner Bjertness seconded the motion and the same being put to a vote, was duly carried.[139]

Within a few days, twenty-four school districts in Marshall and Pennington Counties were dissolved and annexed to the Thief River Falls District as a result of petitioning. More followed in the next few months.

Student and Teacher Lists

The County Line School District was operational from January of 1895 until January of 1956, a total of sixty-one years. Since it both began and ended in the middle of a school year, it was operational for all or parts of sixty-two school years. While there are no student records available for the first fourteen school years, there are for the remaining forty-eight. During that period, the school was closed and students were transported to other districts a total of ten school years: 1926-27, 1929-30, 1930-31, 1949-50, 1950-51, 1951-52, 1952-53, 1953-54, 1954-55, and 1955-56.

This segment of the book lists the names of the County Line students, as well as their teachers, from the 1908-09 school year through the 1948-49 school year. It also includes a chart listing the names of County Line students who were transported to other schools from the 1949-50 school year through the first half of the 1955-56 school year.

Year	Teacher	Students	
1908 - 1909	Abbie Miller	Emil Anderson	Georgia Muzzy
		Ivor Anderson	Lida Muzzy
		Harvey Copp	Banhard Roesnor
		Vivian Copp	Edward Roesnor
		Ada Jacobson	Alice Solem
		Clara Jacobson	Otto Solem
		Annie Johnson	Ruth Solem
		Mary Johnson	Axel Wassgren
		Esther Kellberg	Ingrid Wassgren

Year	Teacher	Students	
1908-09 Con't		Goldie Kellberg Helmer Kellberg Mabel Kellberg	Jennie Wolden Olga Wolden
1909 - 1910	Abbie Miller Irene Caldwell	Emil Anderson Ivor Anderson Willard Andre Harvey Copp Vivian Copp Ada Jacobson Clara Jacobson Annie Johnson Mary Johnson Esther Kellberg Goldie Kellberg Helmer Kellberg Mabel Kellberg	Georgia Muzzy Lida Muzzy Banhard Roesnor Edward Roesnor Alice Solem Arnie Solem Otto Solem Ruth Solem Axel Wassgren Ingrid Wassgren Elsie Wiechmann Grace Wiechmann John Wiechmann
1910 - 1911	Clara Backe	Harvey Copp Vernon Copp Vivian Copp Ada Jacobson Clara Jacobson Esther Kellberg Goldie Kellberg Helmer Kellberg Mabel Kellberg	Leslie Larson Georgia Muzzy Lida Muzzy Emilia Simonson Mabel Simonson Alice Solem Arnie Solem Otto Solem Ruth Solem
1911-1912	Clara Backe	Vernon Copp Vivian Copp Ada Jacobson Bernie Jacobson Clara Jacobson Goldie Kellberg Helmer Kellberg Mabel Kellberg	Leslie Larson Georgia Muzzy Raymond Muzzy Emilia Simonson Mabel Simonson Arnie Solem Otto Solem Ruth Solem

Year	Teacher	Students	
1912 - 1913	Sidona Poston	Vernon Copp Vivian Copp Bernie Jacobson Clara Jacobson Mabel Jacobson Goldie Kellberg	Helmer Kellberg Matilda Liden Georgia Muzzy Raymond Muzzy Arnie Solem Ruth Solem
1913 - 1914	Anna Adolphs	Vernon Copp Vivian Copp Bernie Jacobson Clara Jacobson Mabel Jacobson Goldie Kellberg Helmer Kellberg Julius Liden Matilda Liden	Georgia Muzzy Raymond Muzzy Alfred Solem Arnie Solem Ruth Solem Clarence Williams Cora Williams Harold Williams
1914 - 1915	Mildred Malberg	Lawrence Best Vernon Copp Bernie Jacobson Clara Jacobson Mabel Jacobson Goldie Kellberg Helmer Kellberg Julius Liden	Georgia Muzzy Raymond Muzzy Alfred Solem Arnie Solem Ruth Solem Della Williams Harold Williams
1915 - 1916	Leah Ahlborn	Lawrence Best Lenna Best Vernon Copp Clara Jacobson Mabel Jacobson Goldie Kellberg Julius Liden	Raymond Muzzy Alfred Solem Arnie Solem Ruth Solem Clarence Williams Cora Williams Della Williams

Year	Teacher	Students	
1915-16 Con't		Coral Muzzy Georgia Muzzy	Esther Williams Harold Williams
1916 - 1917	Esther Kellberg	Lawrence Best Lenna Best Vernon Copp Bernie Jacobson Mabel Jacobson Goldie Kellberg Julius Liden	Coral Muzzy Raymond Muzzy Willie Smith Alfred Solem Arnie Solem Della Williams Harold Williams
1917 - 1918	Esther Kellberg	Faye Best Lawrence Best Lenna Best Bernie Jacobson Mabel Jacobson Julius Liden	Coral Muzzy Raymond Muzzy Alfred Solem Della Williams Esther Williams Harold Williams
1918 - 1919	Mabel Kellberg	Faye Best Lawrence Best Lenna Best Bernie Jacobson Emily Jacobson Mabel Jacobson	Leonard Meier Coral Muzzy Raymond Muzzy Alfred Solem Clara Williams Esther Williams
1919 - 1920	Mabel Kellberg	Alvina Amren Esther Amren Hilma Amren Faye Best Lawrence Best Lenna Best Mary Christenson Bernie Jacobson Emily Jacobson	Henry Liden Coral Muzzy Alfred Solem Elvester Stromberg Grace Torreson Alvina Williams Clara Williams Harold Williams
1920 - 1921	Gunda Engen	Alvina Amren Esther Amren Hilma Amren	Coral Muzzy Alfred Solem Allen Solem

Year	Teacher	Students	
1920 - 1921 Con't		Faye Best	Clifford Stromberg
		Lawrence Best	Elvester Stromberg
		Lenna Best	Alvina Williams
		Bernie Jacobson	Clara Williams
		Emily Jacobson	Harold Williams
		Henry Liden	
1921- 1922	Clara Sorenson	Alvina Amren	Henry Liden
		Esther Amren	Coral Muzzy
		Hilma Amren	Allen Solem
		Lawrence Anderson	Clifford Stromberg
		Orrie Anderson	Elvester Stromberg
		Faye Best	Alvina Williams
		Lenna Best	Clara Williams
		Bernie Jacobson	Harold Williams
		Emily Jacobson	
1922 - 1923	Evelyn Saugen	Lawrence Anderson	Coral Muzzy
		Orrie Anderson	Allen Solem
		Faye Best	Clifford Stromberg
		Lenna Best	Elvester Stromberg
		Bernie Jacobson	Alvina Williams
		Emily Jacobson	Clara Williams
		Henry LIden	
1923 - 1924	Inga Hjelle	Hilma Amren	Homer Rustebakke
		Faye Best	Geraldine Shirkey
		Lenna Best	Allen Solem
		Emily Jacobson	Clifford Stromberg
		Henry Liden	Elvester Stromberg
		Coral Muzzy	Alvina Williams
1924 - 1925	Agnes Halvorson	Hilma Amren	Coral Muzzy
		Faye Best	Homer Rustebakke
		Lenna Best	Allen Solem
		Rolland Brooten	Clarence Stromberg

Year	Teacher	Students	
1924-25 Con't		Emily Jacobson Henry Liden	Clifford Stromberg Elvester Stromberg
1925 - 1926	Esther Williams Mrs. Alvin LaSalle	Faye Best Melvin Griebrok Henry Liden	Alvin Rustebakke Homer Rustebakke Allen Solem
1926 - 1927 Classes held at North Star School	Mabel Shefveland	Mary Ann Morben Robert Morben	Alvin Rustebakke Homer Rustebakke
1927- 1928 Classes held at County Line School. North Star transported eight students to County Line.	Ruth Shefveland	Alvin Rustebakke Annette Rustebakke	Homer Rustebakke Alvina Williams
1928 - 1929	Frances Shanahan	Alva Grytdal Edwin Grytdal Perry Grytdal	Alvin Rustebakke Annette Rustebakke Homer Rustebakke Alvina Williams
1929 - 1930 Classes held at Steiner School	Augusta Anderson	Albin Grytdal Alva Grytdal Edwin Grytdal Perry Grytdal	Alvin Rustebakke Annette Rustebakke Homer Rustebakke
1930 - 1931 Classes held at Steiner School	Agnes Koglin	Albin Grytdal Alva Grytdal	Edwin Grytdal Perry Grytdal
1931 - 1932	Margaret Hanson	James Copp Albin Grytdal Alva Grytdal Edwin Grytdal Perry Grytdal	Mildred Jensen Jerold Rude Margaret Rude Myrtle Rude

Year	Teacher	Students	
1932 - 1933	Margaret Hanson	Ardith Copp James Copp Albin Grytdal Edwin Grytdal Perry Grytdal	Duane Jensen Mildred Jensen Jerold Rude Margaret Rude Myrtle Rude
1933 - 1934	Margaret Hanson	Ardith Copp James Copp Albin Grytdal Edwin Grytdal Perry Grytdal Duane Jensen	Mildred Jensen Jerold Rude Margaret Rude Myrtle Rude Curtis Swanson
1934 - 1935	Elizabeth Jorde	Ardith Copp Bernice Copp James Copp Lois Copp Albin Grytdal Perry Grytdal Duane Jensen	Mildred Jensen Arthur Rausch Herman Rausch Joseph Rausch Lawrence Rausch Marie Rausch Curtis Swanson
1935 - 1936	Elizabeth Jorde	Ardith Copp Bernice Copp James Copp Lois Copp Albin Grytdal Duane Jensen Mildred Jensen	Arthur Rausch Herman Rausch Lawrence Rausch Marie Rausch LuVern Smith Curtis Swanson
1936 - 1937	Ethel Kivle	Ardith Copp Bernice Copp James Copp Lois Copp Albin Grytdal Duane Jensen	Arthur Rausch Herman Rausch Lawrence Rausch LuVern Smith Curtis Swanson

Year	Teacher	Students	
1937 - 1938	Ethel Kivle	Ardith Copp Bernice Copp James Copp Lois Copp Duane Jensen Arthur Rausch Helen Rausch	Herman Rausch Lawrence Rausch LuVern Smith Curtis Swanson Bernard Thompson Milton Thompson Norma Thompson
1938 - 1939	Myrtle Starr	James Arras Kenneth Arras Ardith Copp Bernice Copp Lois Copp Duane Jensen Dorothy Muzzy James Muzzy Doris Rausch	Helen Rausch Herman Rausch Lawrence Rausch LuVern Smith Curtis Swanson Senora Swanson Milton Thompson Norma Thompson
1939 - 1940	Myrtle Starr	James Arras Kenneth Arras Ardith Copp Bernice Copp Lois Copp Duane Jensen Dorothy Muzzy James Muzzy Doris Rausch	Helen Rausch Herman Rausch Lawrence Rausch Lowell Rude Rudy Rude LuVern Smith Curtis Swanson Senora Swanson
1940 - 1941	Bernice Halvorson	James Arras Kenneth Arras Bernice Copp Lois Copp Duane Jensen Dorothy Muzzy	Helen Rausch Herman Rausch Lawrence Rausch James Rude Lowell Rude Rudy Rude

Year	Teacher	Students	
1940-41 Con't		James Muzzy	Curtis Swanson
		Doris Rausch	Senora Swanson
1941 - 1942	Bernice Halvorson	James Arras	Helen Rausch
		Kenneth Arras	Lawrence Rausch
		Bernice Copp	James Rude
		Lois Copp	Lowell Rude
		Muriel Copp	Rudy Rude
		Dorothy Muzzy	Curtis Swanson
		James Muzzy	Senora Swanson
		Doris Rausch	
1942 - 1943	Bernice Halvorson	James Arras	James Muzzy
		Kenneth Arras	James Rude
		Bernice Copp	Lowell Rude
		Lois Copp	Arlen Solem
		Muriel Copp	Senora Swanson
		Dorothy Muzzy	
1943 - 1944	Olga Urdahl	Muriel Copp	James Rude
		Marlene Kellberg	Lowell Rude
		Dorothy Muzzy	Arlen Solem
		James Muzzy	Roger Solem
		Marie Nelson	Senora Swanson
		Shirley Nelson	Beverly Urdahl
		Donna Rood	
1944 - 1945	Joyce Meyer	Muriel Copp	Donna Rood
		Marlene Kellberg	James Rude
		James Mattson	Lowell Rude
		Dorothy Muzzy	Arlen Solem
		James Muzzy	Roger Solem
		Marie Nelson	Senora Swanson
		Shirley Nelson	

Year	Teacher	Students	
1945 - 1946	Joyce Meyer	Muriel Copp Philip Jaennette Spencer Johnston Dalys Kellberg Marlene Kellberg Dorothy Muzzy Donna Rood	Janice Rood James Rude Arlen Solem Roger Solem Stuart Solem Senora Swanson
1946 - 1947	Clara Mae Jorde	Muriel Copp Carol Jaennette Philip Jaennette Barbara Johnston Spencer Johnston James Mattson Marilyn Mattson	Dorothy Muzzy Shirley Nelson James Rude Arlen Solem Roger Solem Stuart Solem
1947 - 1948	Clara Mae Jorde	Muriel Copp Carol Jaennette Philip Jaennette Barbara Johnston Spencer Johnston Warren Kron James Mattson	Marilyn Mattson Dorothy Muzzy Shirley Nelson James Rude Arlen Solem Roger Solem Stuart Solem
1948 - 1949	Adeline Everson	Muriel Copp Carol Jaennette Philip Jaennette Gary Mason James Mattson	Marilyn Mattson Shirley Nelson Arlen Solem Roger Solem Stuart Solem

County Line Elementary Students Transported to Other Schools (1949-56)

	Steiner S.D. #17 Marshall County	Lincoln S.D. #18 Pennington County	Knox S.D. #18 Pennington County	Old Washington S.D. #18 Pennington County	Northrop S.D. #18 Pennington County
1949 - 50	Arlen Solem Roger Solem Stuart Solem	Gary Mason	Philip Jaennette Carol Jaennette		
1950 - 51	Roger Solem Stuart Solem Kathryn Solem Robert Rausch		Philip Jaennette Carol Jaennette		
1951 - 52		Philip Jaennette Stuart Solem	Carol Jaennette	Kathryn Solem	Robert Rausch
1952 - 53		Philip Jaennette Stuart Solem Carol Jaennette		Kathryn Solem	Robert Rausch Gary Hoglin Loris Reierson
1953 - 54		Carol Jaennette		Kathryn Solem	Robert Rausch Gary Hoglin Loris Reierson

	Steiner S.D. #17 Marshall County	Lincoln S.D. #18 Pennington County	Knox S.D. #18 Pennington County	Old Washington S.D. #18 Pennington County	Northrop S.D. #18 Pennington County
1954 - 55				Kathryn Solem	Robert Rausch Loris Reierson Judy Reierson Elaine Rodenbo Gerald Rodenbo
1955 - 56				Kathryn Solem	Robert Rausch Loris Reierson Judy Reierson Kermit Solem Donald Rondorf

Note: Steiner held classes for grades one through eight, Lincoln for grades seven through twelve, and Knox, Old Washington, and Northrop for grades one through six.

Teacher Contracts

(Records are unavailable for the years 1894-1908)

School Year	Teacher	Monthly Salary	Length of Contract (in months)	Length of School Year (in months)	Annual Salary
1908-09	Abbie Miller	$ 45	8	8	$ 360
1909-10	Abbie Miller	$ 45	4	8	$ 180
	Irene Caldwell	$ 50	4	8	$ 200
1910-11	Clara Backe	$ 45	8	8	$ 360
1911-12	Clara Backe	$ 50	8	8	$ 400
1912-13	Sidona Poston	$ 50	8	8	$ 400
1913-14	Anna Adolphs	$ 50	8	8	$ 400
1914-15	Mildred Malberg	$ 50	8	8	$ 400
1915-16	Leah Ahlborn	$ 50	8	8	$ 400
1916-17	Esther Kellberg	$ 50	8	8	$ 400
1917-18	Esther Kellberg	$ 55	6	6	$ 330
1918-19	Mabel Kellberg	$ 60	8	8	$ 480
1919-20	Mabel Kellberg	$ 65	8	8	$ 520
1920-21	Gunda Engen	$ 100	8	8	$ 800

School Year	Teacher	Monthly Salary	Length of Contract (in months)	Length of School Year (in months)	Annual Salary
1921-22	Clara Sorenson	$ 100	8	8	$ 800
1922-23	Evelyn Saugen	$ 80	8	8	$ 640
1923-24	Inga Hjelle	$ 85	8	8	$ 680
1924-25	Agnes Halvorson	$ 85	8	8	$ 680
1925-26	Esther Williams	$ 85	6	8	$ 510
	Mrs. Alvin LaSalle	$ 85	2	8	$ 170
1926-27					
1927-28	Ruth Shefveland	$ 90	8	8	$ 720
1928-29	Frances Shanahan	$ 80	8	8	$ 640
1929-30					
1930-31					
1931-32	Margaret Hanson	$ 65	8	8	$ 520
1932-33	Margaret Hanson	$ 65	8	8	$ 520
1933-34	Margaret Hanson	$ 55	8	8	$ 440
1934-35	Elizabeth Jorde	$ 50	8	8	$ 400
1935-36	Elizabeth Jorde	$ 55	8	8	$ 440
1936-37	Ethel Kivle	$ 50	8	8	$ 400
1937-38	Ethel Kivle	$ 55	8	8	$ 440

School Year	Teacher	Monthly Salary	Length of Contract (in months)	Length of School Year (in months)	Annual Salary
1938-39	Myrtle Starr	$ 55	8	8	$ 440
1939-40	Myrtle Starr	$ 55	8	8	$ 440
1940-41	Bernice Halvorson	$ 65	8	8	$ 520
1941-42	Bernice Halvorson	$ 65	8	8	$ 520

The Sixteenth Amendment to the Constitution, passed in 1913, established a federal income tax. Originally only the very wealthy were taxed. That changed in 1942 when Congress passed what was known as "The Victory Tax" to help finance World War II. This tax targeted all workers and was collected by withholding money from their paychecks. The chart below reflects that change.

School Year	Teacher	Monthly Salary	Contract Length (in months)	School Year Length (in months)	Annual Salary
1942-43	Bernice Halvorson	$ 85	8	8	$ 680 - tax
1943-44	Olga Urdahl	$ 95	8	8	$ 760 - tax
1944-45	Joyce Meyer	$ 96.66	12	8	$ 1160 - tax
1945-46	Joyce Meyer	$ 106.66	12	8	$ 1280 - tax
1946-47	Clara Mae Jorde	$ 101.33	12	8	$ 1216 - tax
1947-48	Clara Mae Jorde	$ 120	12	9	$ 1440 - tax
1948-49	Adeline Everson	$ 150	12	9	$ 1800 - tax

School Board List

School Year	Chairman	Treasurer	Clerk
1894-1895			
1895-1896			
1896-1897			
1897-1898	Edward E. Engen	L. E. Erickson	John Finke
1898-1899	Edward E. Engen	John Smith	John Finke
1899-1900	Edward E. Engen	John Smith	John Finke
1900-1901			
1901-1902			
1902-1903			
1903-1904			
1904-1905			
1905-1906			
1906-1907			
1907-1908			
1908-1909			
1909-1910			
1910-1911			
1911-1912			
1912-1913	Peter O. Solem	John Meier	Fred Copp
1913-1914	Peter O. Solem	John Meier	Fred Copp
1914-1915	Peter O. Solem	John Meier	Fred Copp
1915-1916	Peter O. Solem	John Meier	Fred Copp
1916-1917	Peter O. Solem	John Meier	John Christensen
1917-1918	Henry Williams	John Meier	John Christensen

School Year	Chairman	Treasurer	Clerk
1918-1919	Henry Williams	John Meier/ John Kellberg	John Christensen
1919-1920	Henry Williams	John Kellberg	John Christensen/ Peter O. Solem
1920-1921	Hugh Best	John Kellberg	Peter O. Solem
1921-1922	Hugh Best	John Kellberg	Peter O. Solem
1922-1923	Hugh Best	John Kellberg/ Martin Rustebakke	Peter O. Solem
1923-1924	Hugh Best	Martin Rustebakke	Peter O. Solem
1924-1925	Hugh Best	Martin Rustebakke	Peter O. Solem
1925-1926	Hugh Best	Martin Rustebakke	Peter O. Solem
1926-1927	Hugh Best	Martin Rustebakke	Peter O. Solem
1927-1928	Hugh Best	Martin Rustebakke	Vivian Copp
1928-1929	Hugh Best	Martin Rustebakke	Vivian Copp
1929-1930	Alfred Grytdal	Martin Rustebakke	Vivian Copp
1930-1931	Alfred Grytdal	Edwin Swanson	Vivian Copp
1931-1932	Alfred Grytdal	Edwin Swanson	Vivian Copp
1932-1933	Alfred Grytdal	Edwin Swanson	Vivian Copp
1933-1934	Alfred Grytdal	Edwin Swanson	Vivian Copp
1934-1935	Alfred Grytdal	Edwin Swanson	Vivian Copp
1935-1936	Alfred Grytdal	Edwin Swanson	Vivian Copp

School Year	Chairman	Treasurer	Clerk
1936-1937	Alfred Grytdal	Edwin Swanson	Vivian Copp
1937-1938	Alfred Grytdal	Edwin Swanson	Vivian Copp
1938-1939	Math Rausch	Edwin Swanson	Vivian Copp
1939-1940	Math Rausch	Edwin Swanson	Vivian Copp
1940-1941	Math Rausch	Edwin Swanson	Vivian Copp
1941-1942	Helmer Kellberg	Edwin Swanson	Vivian Copp
1942-1943	Helmer Kellberg	Edwin Swanson	Vivian Copp
1943-1944	Helmer Kellberg	Edwin Swanson	Alfred Solem
1944-1945	Helmer Kellberg	Edwin Swanson	Alfred Solem
1945-1946	Helmer Kellberg	Edwin Swanson	Alfred Solem
1946-1947	Ray Rausch	Edwin Swanson	Alfred Solem
1947-1948	Ray Rausch	Edwin Swanson	Alfred Solem
1948-1949	Ray Rausch	Edwin Swanson	Rebecca Solem
1949-1950	Ray Rausch	Edwin Swanson	Rebecca Solem
1950-1951	Ray Rausch	Edwin Swanson	Rebecca Solem
1951-1952	Ray Rausch	Edwin Swanson	Rebecca Solem
1952-1953	Ray Rausch	Curtis Swanson	Rebecca Solem
1953-1954	Ray Rausch	Curtis Swanson	Rebecca Solem
1954-1955	Ray Rausch	Curtis Swanson	Rebecca Solem
1955-1956	Ray Rausch	Curtis Swanson	Rebecca Solem

1920-21 Marshall County School Directory

The directory is a collection of assorted data on the county's one hundred and fifty-seven school districts that existed during the 1920-21 school year. It was the result of a cooperative effort between the Marshall County Superintendent's Office and the Teachers' Patriotic League. Included in the directory is a map of the county and its schools, a list of the school board officers from each district, and a chart of useful information concerning all of the county's one hundred and forty-four one-room country schools.

The cover page lists the names and positions of those who led the countywide teacher organization known as the Teachers' Patriotic League (later changed to the Marshall County Teachers' Association). Among the leaders listed are two teachers with several ties to the County Line School. Mentioned as a sectional leader is Mabel Kellberg, a 1912 graduate of County Line who taught at the school for two years: 1918-19 and 1919-20. Mabel had taken over the teaching position from her sister Esther who had also taught there for two years: 1916-17 and 1917-18.

Another leader mentioned is Amy Whitman, who was serving as president of the organization. Amy was raised on a farm about two and a half miles north of the Kellberg farm, knew the Kellberg family very well, and was a close friend of the Kellberg sisters. Because Amy lived in School District No. 17, she had attended the neighboring Steiner School where she had also taught for two years, 1918-19 and 1919-20, the same two years Mabel was at County Line.

Amy's closest ties with County Line actually happened several years later when her daughter, Joyce Meyer, taught the school for the 1944-45 and 1945-46 school years. While teaching there, Joyce boarded at the Kellberg farm. The farm was now owned by Helmer Kellberg, a brother to Mabel and Esther.

Helmer, a 1915 graduate of County Line, was married to a former County Line teacher named Margaret Hanson, who had taught at the school for three years: 1931-32, 1932-33, and 1933-34.

Such was the life surrounding a country school! Schools functioned as the center of local cultural life, and the lives of those involved became interconnected in a variety of ways, including friendship and marriage.

Helmer and Margaret (Hanson) Kellberg

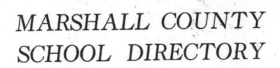

MARSHALL COUNTY
SCHOOL DIRECTORY

OFFICERS

President, Amy Whitman, Warren, R. 4.
Vice-President, Jessie Leslie, Gatzke.
Secretary, Judith Peterson, Alvarado.
Treasurer, Hannah Gjelhaug, Oslo.

CHAIRMEN OF STANDING COMMITTEES

Thrift, Hannah Gjelhaug, Oslo.
Citizenship, Mrs. Charlotte Sheldrew, Grygla.
Health, Eleanor Lee, Grygla.
Improvement, Executive Committee.

Delegate to M. E. A. Meeting at St. Paul, Amy Whitman.

SECTIONS AND LEADERS

Grygla, Roy E. Burhart, Grygla.
Gatzke, Beda Peterson, Rollis.
Middle River, Gaya Olson Middle River.
Holt, Clara E. Larson, Holt.
Strandquist, Ruth Anderson, Strandquist.
Newfolden, Selma Shefveland, Newfolden.
Viking, Hattie Anderson, Viking.
Radium, Bessie Sedlacek, Radium.
Stephen, Anna L. Johnson, Stephen, R. 2.
Argyle, Mable Kellberg, Argyle.
Warren, Amy Whitman, Warren, R. 4.
Oslo and Alvarado, Judith Peterson, Alvarado.

David Johnson, County Superintendent.
Roy E. Luttrell, Assistant.

School Officers of Marshall County

Dist No.	Clerk and P. O. Address	Treasurer and P. O. Address	Chairman and P. O. Address
1	C. R. Gillespie, Stephen	H. I. Yetter, Stephen	B. B. Brett, Stephen
2	Aug. A. Johnson, Warren	Aug. Lundgren, Warren	L. L. Lamberson, Warren
3	W. S. Robertson, Argyle	O. L. Melgaard, Argyle	H. P. Krogh, Argyle
4	Mrs. H. G. Kramer, Radium	John Allen, Radium	Frank Kroll, Radium
5	Adolph Capistran, Stephen	J. W. Olson, Argyle	Aug. Leader, Argyle
6	J. L. Dalquist, Warren	A. P. Nelson, Warren	V. Cederlund, Warren
7	G. H. Palmer, Warren	A. W. Anderson, Warren	Wm. Meyer, Warren
8	Markus Swanson, Oslo	Emil Morberg, Oslo	Christ Johnson, Argyle
9	Aug. G. Hagglund, Alvarado	Ole Bergman, Alvarado	Ole Smith, Alvarado
10	August W. Vieth, Argyle	Henry Kroll, Argyle	Albert Mohn, Argyle
11	Emery Poitras, Argyle	Arthur Riopell, Argyle	Wilfred King, Argyle
12	H. K. Brosdahl, Warren	Albert Metheny, Warren	H. W. Rinkel, Warren
13	Wm. Rickell, Argyle	J. S. Bjorgaard, Argyle	Mike Nowacki, Argyle
14	Knute Jorgensen, Argyle	Ole J. Stanghelle, Argyle	Frank Johnson, Argyle
15	C. J. Gustafson, Strandquist	Louis Torgerson, Strandquist	
16	Ole Olson, Stephen	C. J. Carlson, Stephen	Nels Jensen, Stephen
17	Willis Warring, T. R. Falls	John Whitman, Thief R. Falls	A. C. Simonson, Thief R. Falls
18	O. G. Nelson, Argyle, R. 1, B. 73	Carl Olson, Argyle, R. 1.	Louis Hedquist, Argyle, R. 1
19	Conrad Swanson, Warren, R. 1	Axel J. Lundquist, Warren	P. O. Sward, Alvarado, R. 1
20	M. O. Mattson, Thief River Falls	Fred D. Voth, Thief R. Falls	C. Schwartz, Thief R. Falls
21	Joe Rapacz, Argyle	Male Robertson, Argyle	Alphonse Deschane, Argyle
22	Reuben Kroll, Stephen	Sam Ramiller, Stephen	J. H. Carlson, Stephen
23	F. L. Holter, Oslo	S. O. Hoff, Oslo	C. Tinnes, Oslo
24	C. Emil Anderson, Argyle	C. S. Valin, Argyle	Stanley Rymer, Argyle
25	Adolph Parent, Argyle	Oliver Riopell, Argyle	Leon Schiller, Argyle
26	Lawrence Cormier, Argyle, R. 3	R. A. Marshall, Argyle, R. 3	Henry Schantzen, Stephen
27	Ole Ramon, Oslo, R. 2	Oscar Oseth, Oslo, R. 2	Hiram J. Knutson, Oslo, R. 2
28	John A. Olson, Newfolden, R. 1	John M. Kulseth, Viking	Holterman Olson, Newfolden
29	M. S. Warner, Warren	Christ Olson, Warren	B. Knutson, Warren
30	R. M. Nyhus, Newfolden	M. O. Jarshaw, Newfolden	John Batten, Newfolden
31	F. E. Dahlgren, Alvarado	M. H. Sands, Alvarado	C. O. Olson, Alvarado
32	Albert Berg, Stephen	J. H. Johnson, Stephen	George Benson, Stephen
33	Henry Nelson, Oslo, R. 2	A. J. Slorbakken, Oslo, R. 2	Anton M. Swanson, Alvarado
34	Gilbert T. Grindeland, Newfold.	Louis Thompson, Newfolden	John Halvorsen, Viking
35	D. B. Bakke, Holt	C. H. Gunheim, Holt	T. E. Ellestad, Holt
36	Emil Holmgren, Warren	Axel Swanson, Warren	Carl A. Johnson, Warren
37	G. W. Nelson, Viking	John Nelson, Viking	C. A. Lindell, Viking
38	Carl G. Gustafson, Viking	Claus A. Johnson, Viking	Emmet Larson, Viking
39	O. O. McCurdy, Newfolden	A. F. Holmaas, Newfolden	Anton Hanson, Newfolden
40	Carl Skurdahl, Warren	V. M. Johnson, Warren	Dudley Cheney, Warren
41	Alex Hillquist, Rosewood	Joel Sjoberg, Rosewood	Swen Swenson, Rosewood
42	J. W. Mapps, Warren	Erick Anderson, Warren	A. J. Hall, Warren
43	Logen Conner, Stephen	Chas. Thibodo, Stephen	Theo. Smith, Stephen
44	John Gratzek, Strandquist	Wm. Berrurez, Strandquist	Ignacy Zakrzewski, Strandquist
45	G. Torkelson, Strandquist	Karl Torkelson, Strandquist	Ole Sjodin, Strandquist
46	Paul Krough, Stephen	Emery Dufault, Stephen	Archie Poitras, Stephen
47	Arnold V. Dahlberg, Newfolden	Otto W. Anderson, Newfolden	John Arthur Anderson, Newfolden
48	Will Rinkenberger, Stephen	Louis Roy, Stephen	Herman Knoll, Stephen
49	Ole Kleppe, Newfolden	H. E. Myhre, Newfolden	Carl Hanson, Newfolden
50	Robert Setterholm, Argyle, R. 3	A. J. Lindstrom, Argyle, R. 3	A. J. Lindquist, Argyle, R. 3
51	Alb. Buro, Fork	I. Arness, Fork	Emil Hegman, Fork
52	E. O. Hjelle, Newfolden	A. S. Rokke, Newfolden	Alfred Elseth, Newfolden
53	John H. Tuura, Middle River	Otto Krane, Middle River	O. I. Olson, Middle River
54	Henry Hamann, Stephen	C. Soderland, Stephen	Chas. Peterson, Stephen
55	John R. Price, Stephen	S. Price, Stephen	Carl Benson, Stephen
56	Ole J. Westman, Viking, R. 1	Levi Johnson, Argyle, R. 1	S. E. Sloan, Viking
57	A. E. Carlson, Radium	P. J. Turnlund, Radium	Ernest Otto, Viking
58	E. A. Erickson, Holt	Chas. Skoglund, Holt	Ed. Erickson, Holt
59	J. A. Sorum, Holt	Louis Wegre, Holt	Ole J. Lunke, Holt
60	Fridolph Dahlin, Holt, R. 1	Chas. Standberg, Argyle, R. 2	Louis Larson, Argyle, R. 2
61	August Nass, Holt, R. 1	T. B. Folden, Holt, R. 1	H. O. Ekerdalen, Holt, R. 1
62	Albert Oberg, Argyle, R. 4	Ole Tverstal, Argyle, R. 2	Ola Leden, Argyle, R. 2
63	H. S. Thibodo, Stephen	M. C. Rud, Stephen	C. J. Rud, Stephen
64	Henry B. Severts, Middle River	George C. Breese, Middle River	Ed. Black, Middle River
65	Arthur Flygare, Strandquist	J. J. Oistad, Strandquist	Louis Anderson, Strandquist

240

School Officers of Marshall County

Dist No.	Clerk and P. O. Address	Treasurer and P. O. Address	Chairman and P. O. Address
66	Gust Johnson, Drayton, N. Dak.	Peter Person, Drayton, N. D.	J. T. Danielson, Drayton, N. D.
67	O. L. Brekkestran, Newfolden	Mathias Seielstad, Newfolden	A. C. Gast, Newfolden
68	Louis Roseland, Newfolden	Chr. Shefveland, Newfolden	Erick B. Johnson, Newfolden
69	M. L. Ihle, Newfolden	Lars Bjorsness, Newfolden	John Hasseth, Newfolden
70	Thos. Frederick, Stephen	Andrew Olson, Stephen	Erik T. Rhodes, Stephen
71	A. P. Appelquist, Warren	Alfred Horgen, Warren	H. L. Palmer, Warren
72	Peter Solem, Thief River Falls	John Kelberg, Thief R. Falls	Hugh Best, Thief R. Falls
73	John Olberg, Middle River	Anna Olberg, Middle River	A. V. Johnson, Middle River
74	C. A. Anderson, Middle River	Albin T. Anderson, Mid. River	Wm. Johnson, Middle River
75	Napoleon Beaudry, Stephen	Martin Nelson, Stephen	A. Bedard, Stephen
76	Paul Stock, Thief River Falls	Frank Kains, Mavie	C. H. Struble, Mavie
77	Thos. McGlynn, Stephen	G. K. Fodness, Stephen	Gert Heggen, Stephen
78	Leo Eagan, Pork	Pat Copps, Oslo	Fred Cronkhite, Oslo
80	Ben Arrends, Gatzke	Ernest G. Johnson, Gatzke	Carl Knutson, Gatzke
81	Otto Johnson, Jane	M. J. Polansky, Jane	Telford Anderson, Jane
82	Gustav Berg, Gatzke		
83	Tollef Skramstad, Middle River	Chas. Hanson, Middle River	Enok Skramstad, Mid. River
84	J. A. Russell, Thief River Falls	Gunne Ose, Thief River Falls	Gunston Skomedal, T. R. F.
85	W. C. Skeels, Rollis	Peter Czek, Rollis	Dell Huartson, Rollis
86	M. C. Anderson, Oslo, R. 1	M. H. Linderoth, Alvarado	C. A. Hamerlund, Oslo, R. 2
87	Lars Oina, Karlstad	A. H. Lund, Karlstad	J. R. Haskin, Karlstad
88	A. B. Carlson, Warren	O. K. Kvale, Warren	O. Myrfield, Warren
89	Palmer Lund, Gatzke	Simon T. Rue, Grygla	Otto Haack, Sr., Grygla
91	J. H. Clausen, Germantown	F. J. Cummings, Germantown	J. J. Kast, Germantown
92	S. M. Haugen, Strandquist	Mrs. V. Holmstrom, Strandquist	J. E. Holmstrom, Strandquist
93	G. O. Hanson, Strathcona	Helen Rankin, Middle River	G. H. Omlid, Middle River
94	Oscar Tveten, Grygla	Noldus L. Nelson, Grygla	Anund Norby, Grygla
95	Sam Anderson, Grygla	Andrew Morken, Grygla	Olaf Leshar, Grygla
96	T. Thorkildson, Stephen	Sol Lundin, Stephen	Fred Field, Stephen
97	Norbert W. Sinnott, Stephen	John Whalen, Stephen	John J. Lind, Stephen
98	Jas. Cullen, Goodridge	Otto Keisow, Goodridge	Carl Erickson, Goodridge
99	Joseph A. Vary, Stephen	Philias Vary, Stephen	Olaf Rood, Argyle
100	G. E. Gibson, Newfolden	Nels Stongberg, Newfolden	Jacob Sjogren, Newfolden
101	H. E. Elseth, Jevne	Albert Gjovik, Jevne	B. T. Roppe, Jevne
102	Ole Banken, Strathcona	S. O. Hoff, Jevne	Ole Jevne, Strathcona
103	Ole A. Winson, Gatzke	E. E. Engevig, Gatzke	Carlot C. Tale, Gatzke
104	C. O. Taylor, Jevne	Knute K. Haugh, Jevne	J. A. Blewett, Jevne
105	A. Hodik, Benwood	Thos. Ellefson, Homolka	Wm. Stephenson, Benwood
106	Hans Bjornerud, Argyle R. 3	Emaniue Andeen, Argyle, R. 1	Alfred Willer, Argyle, R. 1
107	John L. Johnson, Newfolden	Carl Amundson, Newfolden	N. O. Lausness, Strandquist
108	A. O. Aspelin, Randen	P. A. Westberg, Randen	O. J. Berglund, Aspelin
109	Paul P. Sund, Esplee	J. E. Ballou, Esplee	Ed. Martinson, Esplee
110	L. P. Poppenhagen, Goodridge	E. W. Peterson, Goodridge	Martin Westby, Goodridge
111	Miss Emma Sjoquist, Strandquist	Maria J. Bernhardson, Strandquist	Ole Wangen, Strandquist
112	Silas Torgerson, T. R. Falls	Jacob Klungnes, T. R. Falls	R. Storm, Thief River Falls
113	Albin E. Lofquist, Strandquist	N. E. Lofquist, Strandquist	Emanuel Nelson, Strandquist
114	Andrew B. Olson, Karlstad	Lewis Westlund, Strathcona	Thos. Braaten, Strathcona
115	A. J. Anderson, Grygla	H. T. Peterson, Grygla	O. J. Johnson, Grygla
116	J. Leverson, Grygla	Hans Hanson, Grygla	Chas. Buholz, Grygla
117	G. A. Sustad, Viking, R. 1	A. O. Brink, Viking, R. 1	Chas. Peterson, Viking, R. 1
118	John Ristau, Thief River Falls	H. P. Nabben, Thief R. Falls	Hans Jorstad, T. R. Falls
119	Mrs. Magda Blakkestad, Goodridge	John Graff, Goodridge	W. M. Jones, Goodridge
120	H. E. Longevan, Goodridge	J. H. Roller, Germantown	Ole P. Nelson, Germantown
121	Christ Nelson, Thief River Falls	Sam Groven, T. R. Falls	Victor Trachman, T. R. Falls
122	Carl T. Olson, Randen	Andrew Olson, Randen	Ole S. Jevning, Homolka
123	Mrs. M. Haroldson, Gatzke	M. N. Nelson, Gatzke	K. Knutson, Gatzke
124	Alfred Norlund, Homolka	John Pearson, Homolka	Peter Norlund, Homolka
125	J. C. Figenskau, Olso	J. A. Hilden, Oslo	R. A. Hallquist, Oslo
126	C. A. Berg, Middle River	E. P. Modin, Middle River	R. D. V. Carr, Middle River
127	Hartvik Engen, Vking, R. 1	Lars Akre, Viking, R. 1	Oscar Shern, Viking, R. 1
128	Ingvart Dahl, Randen	Hans Dahl, Randen	
130	Ben Eliason, Strandquist	P. E. Sihlberg, Strandquist	Victor Lefrooth, Strandquist
131	Carl Thompson, Radium	Louis J. Hill, Radium	Anton Zink, Radium
132	Joe McGregor, Radium	Wm. Potucek, Warren	Chas. Potucek, Warren
133	A. G. Loftness, Thief River Falls	Carl Jorde, Thief River Falls	Peter Hornseth, T. R. Falls
134	Alfred Hvidsten, Stephen	John Williams, Stephen	Frank Kuznia, Stephen
135	Helmer P. Bjerken, Germantown	Halvor Sollid, Germantown	Halvor Tweten, Germantown
136	Anton J. Osen, Goodridge	Anton Knutson, Goodridge	N. T. Jorgenson, Goodridge
137	S. S. Sorenson, Newfolden	Christ Evenson, Newfolden	J. J. Serbus, Newfolden
138	J. S. Gajeski, Argyle, R. 3	J. F. Lindstrom, Strandquist	Andrew Voytila, Strandquist
139	S. H. Sandland, Grygla	Carl Sulland, Grygla	G. O. Sandland, Grygla
140	Hartvig Hanson, Jevne	Ole A. Berg, Newfolden	Hans Bursvold, Jevne
141	Arthur Johnson, Middle River	Mat Brandon, Middle River	Egbert Johnson, Middle River
142	C. P. Haugen, Newfolden	T. Karlstad, Newfolden	Hans Haugen, Newfolden
143	Adolph Klenk, Holt	Mrs. William Koepp, Holt	Herman Niemela, Holt
144	Christ L. Rud, Viking	Henry Sustad, Viking	Oscar Drotts, Viking
145	A. S. Bernstein, Golden Valley	Clarence Larson, Golden Valley	Edwin Johnson, Golden Valley
146	Ole Maakstad, Golden Valley	Peter Ostlund, Golden Valley	Issac Ostlund, Golden Valley
147	Chas. J. Berg, Jane	John Henning, Jane	Hans Larson, Jane
148	A. C. Jahr, Holt	Palmer P. Peterson, Holt	H. P. Peterson, Holt
149	E. V. Wickwire, Middle River	Geo. W. Curtiss, Middle River	Mrs. E. V. Wickwire, Mid. Ri.
150	Mrs. E. M. Evans, Newfolden	Robert E. Evans, Newfolden	Erick Petterson, Newfolden
151	John L. Anderson, Rollis	M. Leiran, Rollis	Elon Nauman, Rollis
152	Casper J. Dale, Holt	Christ Norbeck, Golden Valley	J. S. Gabrielson, Golden Valley
153	Edwin Wahlin, Goodridge	Andrew Furagen, Goodridge	Ed. Kivle, Goodridge
154	Ole Sparby, Gatzke	Nels Satre, Gatzke	Clara Wold, Gatzke
155	Mrs. W. S. Wright, Rollis	Erick Hill, Rollis	F. W. Lassila, Rollis
157	O. G. Tharaldson, Germantown	Algot Johnson, T. R. Falls	Alex Magee, Germantown
158	S. G. Svenkeson, Holt	Fred Peterson, Holt	Ole Christenson, Holt
159	Albert Klunghes, Thief R. Falls	Soren Moe, Thief River Falls	G. A. Soiney, T. R. Falls
160	Wm. Rasmussen, Strandquist	Swan Odson, Strandquist	Isaac Isaacson, Strandquist
161	Tom Simonson, Viking, R. 1	Lonnie Hanson, Viking, R. 1	Harold Hanson, Viking, R. 1

ONE ROOM RURAL SCHOOLS

District No.	Name of School	Location: Section	Location: Township	Distance in miles from School to R. R. Station	Class of State Aid	No. Months School 1920-21	Enrollment 1920-21	Monthly Salary of Teacher 1920-21	Janitor Service furnished by the Board: Fires, No. Months	Sweeping, No. Mos.	Scrub. times pr. yr.	Paid to Teacher in excess of salary	Distance in Miles from School to Boarding place	Cost of Room and Board per month	Boarding Place 1920-21
5-N	Sunshine	20	Wanger	8	A	8	16	$ 95	3		8	$	¾	$23.00	Adolph Capistran
5-S		32	Wanger			8		115							
6-S	Honorville	20	Warrenton	5½	A	8	19	115	0	0	4		1	25.00	J. L. Dahlquist
7	Cook	12	Warrenton	1	A	8	28	115	7		8		¾	20.00	Aug. W. Anderson
8	Lincoln	34	Big Woods	10	A	8	15	100	3		8		1		Emil Morberg
9	North Star	30	Vega	3	A	8	22	90					1		
10		22	Bloomer	8	A	9	18	100	2		8		1	28.00	Aug. Pagnac
12		29	Foldahl	6	A	9	20	110	3	0	8		2	25.00	Matt. Lindbeck
13	West School	10	Alma	6	A	8	38	100			16	5.00	⅛	24.00	Mike Nowacki
14		23	Alma			8		100							
15	Woodside	8	Nelson Park	8	B	8	15	90	3		8	5.00	⅛	20.00	Ole Erickson
16	Augsburg	8	Augsburg	12	A	8	30	125	5		8			20.00	Louis Schmidt
17	Steiner	28	Excel	⅛	A	8	20	100	6	6	8		1	25.00	J. P. Swanson
18	Poplar Grove	30	Alma	4½	A	8	16	100	6	6	8		¾	16.00	Oscar G. Swanson
19-E		11	Vega			8		95							
19-W	West	5	Vega	5½	A	8	32	95	6	0	8		1	16.00	Seth Erickson
21		13	Middle River			8		75							
22	West	20	Sinnott	3	A	9	12	90					½	20.00	H. Peterson
24		30	Middle River	4½	A	9	14	110	4	0	8			20.00	Leon Goulet
25		5	Middle River	3½		9	36	125	9		8		¾	20.00	Oliver Riopelle
26	Lincoln	25	Tamarac	6	A	9	7	100	7		8		1½	20.00	P. T. Curtin
27	Big Woods	29	Big Woods	8½	B	8	25	100	4		8		1¼		Mrs. Maria Gjelhaug
28	Edgewood	17	New Solum	6	B	7	15	105	7	7	10	5.00	¾	25.00	F. Hodik
30	Sunshine	2	New Solum	5	B	7	12	95	3		8		1½	25.00	L. L. Roseland
33-W		9	Oak Park	5½		8	26	90	3		8		¾	24.00	K. S. Overlid
33-E		10	Oak Park	8	A	8	33	90	5		8		¼	15.00	Albert Knutson
34			New Solum			8		100							
36	Holmgren	26	Vega	1	A	8	17	90	6		8		½	16.00	Alex N. Swanson
38		10	Viking	3½	A	8	17	105	6	0	16		½	18.00	C. A. Johnson
39	Popple Lane	26	Marsh Grove	6	B	7	18	90	6		8		2	22.00	O. O. McCurdy
41		3	New Solum					115							
42		35	McCrea	4½	A	9	21	120	5	5	8		1¼	26.00	John W. Mapps
43		22	Eagle Point	13½	B	8	23	85	8		6	7.00	¾	20.00	Chas. Thibodo
44	Florian	8	Wright	12	B	7	42	125	7	7	8		⅛	30.00	Mrs. Marie Kovers
45	Fir School	11	Nelson Park	5		7	15	80	3		9		⅛	15.00	Gunval Torkelson
46		29	Tamarac	4½	B	6	10	100	6	6	8		4½	20.00	J. E. Beaudry
47		30	Spruce Valley					100							
48	Road Way	30	Tamarac	5		8	19	95	3		8		1½	16.00	Herman Kroll
50		24	Wanger	12	A	8	36	125	5		8		¾	20.00	Mrs. Gust Anderson
51		29	Fork			8	8	120							
52		28	West Valley	9	A	7	22	110	5	0	7		¾	18.00	E. O. Hjelle
53		18	Cedar			8	20	110							
54	Parker	2	Parker	4		9	6	85	4	4	3		1	20.00	Chas. Peterson
55	Golden Glow	26	Augsburg	10	B	7	18	90			14			20.00	T. Mulvey
56		22	Foldahl	5	A	8	20	115	3		8		2	20.00	Ole Westman
57		11	Comstock			8		100							
58		58	Holt	7	B	7	25	120	0	0	7		7	24.00	John Udstrand
59	Sunnyside	25	Holt	3½	A	8	25	125	0	0	8		0		
60	Bloomwood	13	Big Woods	10	A	8	14	100	6		16		1¼	20.00	Alfred Lindberg
61	Pioneer	17	Holt	3½	A	8	32	115	2	2	8		⅛	22.00	Mrs. Ellefson
62		11	Big Woods			7	12	120							
64	Honor Bright	8	Cedar	4	A	8	20	100	6	0	8		½	20.00	A. A. Peterson
66	Plainview	10	Eagle Point	5½	A	8	17	90	5	0	8		1	20.00	J. P. Danielson
67		8	Marsh Grove			8	20	110							
68	Lincoln	25	Newfolden	4	B	7	15	95	5	5	8		1¼	20.00	Chr. Shefveland
69	Wildwood	20	Newfolden	3½	A	8	22	90	8	0	8		1¾	25.00	Martin Tunheim
70	Donelly	32	Donelly	5	A	9	14	125	3		8		¾	25.00	Ward Field
71	Horgen	14	McCrea	5	A	9	20	100	5	0	8		1¼		H. L. Palmer
72	County Line	8	Excel	5	A	8	17	100	0	0	4		1½		Christ Engen
74		27	Spruce Valley	2¾	B	8	20	110	0	0	8		½	20.00	C. A. Anderson
75		9	Fork	12	A	8	13	110	6	6	8		1¾	15.00	Jno. McGlynn
76	Independence	32	Grand Plain	5	A	8	31	95	3	0	8		¼	22.50	Chas. H. Struble
77	McGlynn	7	Parker	8	A	8	14	130	0	0	16		1	25.00	G. Heggen
78	Oak Point	8	Big Woods	12½	B	7	19	120	3	0	8		1	35.00	I. J. Amundson
80		9	Rollis	18	B	7	19	90	6	0	7		1¼	23.00	Ben Arends
81		11	Whiteford				17	115							
82-S	Pleasant View	23	Rollis	21	A	8	24	110	4	0	8		¼	25.00	P. Wolden
82-N		11	Rollis	21	A	8	15	110	6	0	8		1	20.00	Wm. Kelley
84	Riverside	27	Excel	2	A	8	16	100	3	0	8		¼	25.00	John Skomedal

ONE ROOM RURAL SCHOOLS

District No.	Name of School	Location: Section	Location: Township	Distance in miles from School to R. R. Station	Class of State Aid	No. Months School 1920-21	Enrollment 1920-21	Monthly Salary of Teacher 1920-21	Janitor Service furnished by the Board: Fires, No. Months	Janitor Service furnished by the Board: Sweeping, No. Mos.	Janitor Service furnished by the Board: Scrub. times pr. yr.	Paid to Teacher in excess of salary	Distance in Miles from School to Boarding place	Cost of Room and Board per month	Boarding Place 1920-21.
85	Rollis	21	Rollis	18	A	8	17	125	6	0	8		⅛	20.00	W. S. Williams
86		3	Oak Park	8	A	8	15	90	0	0	16		1½		N. L. Hanson
87		5	East Park	7	A	8	18	110	5	0	8		¾	20.00	T. Duvos
88	Lincoln	8	McCrea	5½	A	8	29	90	3	0	8		¼	22.00	Elmer Brown
89		26	Eckvoll			8		100							
91		12	Grand Plain	8		7	12	85	4	0	7		⅛	25.00	Ludwig Rosette
92	Oak Ridge	24	Wright	9	B	7	20	100	7	0	8		1¼	20.00	Lars Barstad
93		8	Como	9	A	8	14	100	6	0			1¼	28.00	Joseph M. Rankin
94	Glenwood	11	Valley	25		8	22	90	0	0	8		0	20.00	
95		8	Valley	25		8	10	110							
96	Happy Corner	11	Sinnott	9	A	8	17	110	0	0	8		½	24.00	Fred Field
97		8	Sinnott			9		90							
98		25	Moylan					100							
99	Acme	25	Fork	13		8	4	100	0	0	0		¾	24.00	Fred Christenson
100		8	New Maine			7		90							
101		25	East Park	8		6	16	122	8		8	3.00	½	20.00	Albert Gjovik
102		19	Huntly			6		90							
103		18	Veldt			7		110							
104		11	New Maine					100							
106		8	Foldahl			8		115							
107	Woodland	27	West Valley	7½	B	7	10	95	4		8		1¼	22.00	Halvor Amundson
108	Elm Park	27	Linsell	28	B	7	15	85	7	7	8		2	20.00	Robert Alstrom
109	East	26	Espelie	14	A	8	20	95	8	8	8		¾	22.00	Peter Carlson
109	West	20	Espèlie	11	A	8	11	95	8	3	8	5.00	¾	20.00	Paul P. Sund
111		30	East Park	4	A	8	10	100	8	0	8		4	25.00	P. Wikstrom
113		30	Nelson Park			8		115							
114	East	3	Huntly	2	B	7	24	90	0	0	8		½	24.00	John Johnson
114	West	6	Huntly			7		85							
116		2	Espelie			8		90							
117		32	Viking	2½		7	19	95	5	0	8		1	20.00	G. A. Sustad
118	Flo	35	Agder	3½	B	7	22	125	4	0	8		½	22.00	B. Antonson
119		31	Moylan			8		120							
120		35	Grand Plain			8		100							
121	Sunnyside	32	Agder	3	B	7	32	110	0	0	8		2		Mr. Greibrok
122	Hazel Hill	13	Moose River	22	0	6	17	85	6	6	6		2½	20.00	Robert Alstrom
123		35	Moose River			6		120							
124		18	Moose River			7		65							
127	Green Valley	29	Marsh Grove	7	B	8	24	100	6	0	8		1¼	20.00	Iver Haarstad
128	Elm Park	19	Linsell	22		6	17	85	6	6	6		2½	20.00	
130	Sunnyside	4	West Valley	3	A	8	26	100	4	0	8		1	20.00	P. O. Hanson
131	Meadow Lawn	3	Comstock	5½	B	7	27	115	7		8		1	24.00	Tony Ruff
132	McGregor	8	Comstock	3	B	8	9	85	3		8		¼	20.00	Joe McGregor
133		2	Excel	5		7	18	73	0	0	2		1½		Jorgen H. Sannes
134	Prairie View	8	Wanger	8	A	8	25	95	6	0	8		1¼	23.00	Adolph Capistran
135		32	Evkvoll					115							
137		14	New Solum					96							
138		28	Wright	13	B	7	26	125	5	0	7		2¼	25.00	Mrs. Christ Solum
139	Edgewood	28	Valley	20	B	7	24	80	2	0	7		1	14.00	G. O. Sandland
140	Goodwill	20	New Maine	6		8	16	85	3	0	8		¼	15.00	
141		35	Como	6		8	16	85	3	0	8		¼	15.00	Egbert Johnson
142	Sunnyside	11	Marsh Grove	4	A	8	18	100	0	0	7		1-5	24.00	Tom Kolstad
143	Koepp	30	Cedar	6	B	8	35	100	0	0	8		0		
144		2	Viking	2	A	8	15	90	4	4	8		¾	20.00	Oscar Drotts
145	Bernstein	11	Mud Lake	17	A	8	12	125	3	0			1¼	25.00	Edwin Johnson
147	Cozy Nook	28	Thief Lake	14		6	15	100	0	0	6		¾	20.00	Hans Larson
148		33	East Valley	9	A	8	23	130	0	0	8		0		
149		18	Whiteford	11	A	9	12	100	0	0	9		¼	15.00	E. V. Wickwire
150		7	Spruce Valley	3	B	7	27	100	0	0	7		0	15.00	E. M. Evans
151		27	Whiteford			8		80							
152	Wilson	9	Mud Lake	15	A	8	20	125	0	0	0				
153	Woodrow	7	Espelie			7		105							
154	Plainview	29	Veldt	25	B	8	15	105	0	0	0			20.00	
155		8	Eckvoll			8		125							
158		10	East Valley			7		120							
159		8	Agder			7		100							
160	Oakdale	22	Nelson Park	5	B	7	18	100	0	0	7		¼	25.00	Victor Erickson
161		5	Viking			8		100							

SEMI-GRADED SCHOOLS

District No.	Name of School	Location	Distance in miles from School to R. R. Station	No. Months School 1920-21	Enrollment 1920-21	Principal Salary	Prim. Dept. Salary	Fires, No. Months	Sweeping, No. Mos.	Scrubbing, times per year	Paid to Teacher in excess of salary	Cost of Room and Board per month	Boarding Place
4	Radium	Radium	0	8	60	$110	$105	8	8	8	----	$28	Mr. Sedlacek J. H. Loen
37	Viking	Viking	0	8	52	110	100	8	0	8	----	20	Oscar L. Gustafson
115	Grygla	Grygla	20	9	45	125	85	--	--	9	----		

TWO-ROOM CONSOLIDATED SCHOOL

40	Boxville	Warrenton Twp. near Warren—Sec. 5	5	9	25	$125	$100	9	7	9	----	$22 20	D. O. Cheney G. I. Skurdahl

GRADED CONSOLIDATED SCHOOLS

Dist.	Location	Superintendent	Grade Teachers	H. S. Teachers
31	Alvarado	Sedate M. Brown	4	4
35	Holt	Emil Prushek	4	Same teachers
49	Newfolden	O. W. Yngve	4	2
65	Strandquist	Geo. L. Netteland	3	2
125	Oslo	Lester Skamfer	4	2
126	Middle River	M. W. Holtsapple	4	4

HIGH SCHOOLS AND GRADED SCHOOLS

Dist.	Location	Superintendent	Grade Teachers	H. S. Teachers
1	Stephen	H. L. Bleecker	4	5
2	Warren	G. Holmquist	9	10
3	Argyle	A. C. Pederson	5	5

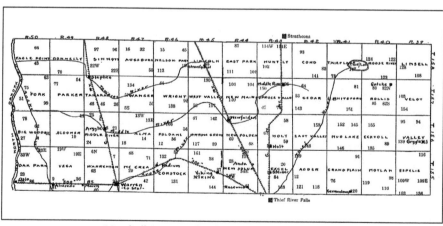

Marshall County School District Map, 1920-1921

1942-43 County Line Log

During the 1942-43 school year, the County Line teacher, Bernice Halvorson, had her students publish a semi-monthly student log. The log's focus was on the day-to-day activities of the school, but it also dealt with other matters of interest within the neighborhood. The following is a condensed version of their works with only the school related issues included.

*****

"This week we started selling War Stamps. We sold for $1.40."

"All over the United States the pupils of all the schools have started a Junior Scrap Army. Our slogan is 'Save Scrap to Lick a Jap.' Our officers and their duties are: Captain, Miss Halvorson - to assign places and arranging transportation of the scrap; Lieutenant, Kenneth Arras - to keep the books; Sergeant, Lowell Rude - to weigh the scrap and fix boxes for tinfoil, brass, and so on; Corporal, James Arras - to sort the scrap."

"Arlen Solem started school this fall."

"All the pupils of the County Line School are members of the American Junior Red Cross."

"Everyone in school has had perfect attendance so far!"

"Mrs. Swanson and Mrs. Arras visited school on October 14th. We'd like to see more mothers come."

Eighth Grade Class
October 16, 1942

*****

"We sold War Stamps for $1.70 on October 21st. This week the sale of stamps came to $1.20."

"The Arras family moved to Thief River Falls on Wednesday of last week. The pupils and teacher had a farewell party for Kenneth and Jim on Wednesday and gave them each a gift of remembrance."

"On November 6th we are having open house at our school. A blanket is to be given away, Bingo will be played, and lunch will be served. Everyone come and bring your friends!"

"Visitors at school on Thursday afternoon, October 20th, were Mrs. Alfred Solem, Lloyd Halvorson, and Miss Lockrem."

"A Halloween party was had at the schoolhouse on Friday afternoon. Noisemakers, masks, and games added to the fun. The little folks who visited were Marlene and Dalys Kellberg and Roger and Stuart Solem."

Eighth Grade Class
October 30, 1942

*****

"On Friday night, November 6th, we had open house. We had a short program at the beginning. After the program, we sold tickets on a blanket, sold candy and gum, passed the grab box, and played Bingo. Senora Swanson was the lucky winner of the blanket. At the close of the evening, we had lunch. We took in $30.05 and cleared $20.85."

"The stamp sale on November 4th was $2.10. The sale on November 11th was $1.10."

"On Armistice Day, all the pupils made patriotic posters."

"We have new draperies to brighten up the schoolroom."

"We have a Junior Citizens' League meeting every two weeks. The officers for the last two weeks were: police, James Muzzy; outdoor committee, girls - Bernice Copp, boys - James Rude; board cleaner, Lowell Rude; housekeeper, Lois Copp; waste paper basket passer, Dorothy Muzzy. We elect officers to take care of the meetings every fourth meeting. Those serving now are: President, Lois Copp; Vice President, Lowell Rude; Secretary, James Muzzy; Treasurer, Lois Copp. The treasurer has the job all year."

"We have cooks to warm hot lunches and wash dishes. First week cooks were Bernice Copp and Senora Swanson. This week they are James Muzzy and Lowell Rude."

"We got new reading and health books last week. There are some for every grade."

"Those who have had perfect attendance are Arlen Solem, Dorothy Muzzy, James Muzzy, Senora Swanson, Bernice Copp, and Lois Copp."

Eighth Grade Class
November 13, 1942

*****

"On November 24th we had a Thanksgiving party at the school. We had a little program put on by the pupils. The parents and pupils played games after the program. Lunch was served later."

"Our Christmas program is going to be on the night of December 19th. You are all invited to come."

"The fifth, sixth, and eighth grades wrote letters to their parents on how to prevent colds and how to take care of yourself if you do get a cold."

"The War Stamp sale on November 24th was $2.65; on December 2nd, $1.00; and on December 9th, $1.40."

"There has been a diphtheria scare. Some of the pupils have been inoculated. Bernice and Muriel have been home from school with sore arms."

"We have been having cheese and apples which we get through the Nutrition Program for Schools."

"We have put up the curtains and some decorations in the school for the Christmas program."

"Arlen Solem missed school today. Those who have had perfect attendance so far are Lois Copp and James Muzzy."

"Bernice Copp was back in school today after staying out because of her inoculation."

"Miss Judith Lockrem, our superintendent, and Miss Iva Howe visited school for a short time this afternoon."

Eighth Grade Class
December 11, 1942

*****

"Kenneth and Dale Ranum visited school on Wednesday, January 6th."

"Lois Copp and James Muzzy are the only ones who have perfect attendance since school started."

"Our school started the fourth of January, after a two-week vacation."

"We took in $2.10 for defense stamps on January 6, 1943. On December 16, 1942, we took in $1.20."

"Muriel Copp has not been in school after Christmas vacation. Bernice has not been in school since last Monday. We have not seen the Rude children since vacation. This means there has not been a big school week."

"We have made memory gem booklets to which we add a new gem almost every week."

"We only had two weeks of Christmas vacation this year."

"Mr. Swanson came after Senora a bit early today because of the bad storm."

"Lois Copp was the owner of the most points at the close of the 'Extra Reports' contest in the upper grades."

"It has been very hard to keep the floor in the schoolhouse warm enough."

"Mr. Jeannette came for Dorothy and James with the tractor about 3:30 this afternoon. Lois Copp was excused then too, since she was the only pupil left in school."

Eighth Grade Class
January 8, 1943

*****

"We took in $2.60 for defense stamps on February 3rd. For the three preceding weeks, the amounts were $2.30, $1.40, and $1.20."

"On one of the sideboards, Lowell Rude and James Muzzy have made a chalk drawing of Abraham Lincoln's home."

"We are learning about the signs and notes in music."

"When the weather is nice, we slide down a big snow hill on skis."

"School was dismissed a bit early on Monday because Miss Halvorson was an attendant at a wedding that evening in town."

"There have been three days since vacation that there were no pupils in school because of the bad weather."

"The County Line Log was not put out two weeks ago because the cold weather kept the pupils at home."

Eighth Grade Class
February 5, 1943

*****

"The large snowbank has gotten very big during these last storms. The bank, which is between the woodshed and the schoolhouse, makes a good slide."

"Dorothy Muzzy was absent all last week because of a toothache and the cold weather."

"Lois Copp visited at the Swanson home a few Sundays ago. Senora took a picture of her on horseback."

"We have a new oilcloth to cover the kerosene stove."

"For the defense stamp sale, we took in $1.70 last Wednesday. This week we took in $1.20."

"Muriel Copp was not in school on March 8th because of the cold weather."

"There will be no school on Friday, March 12th, because of the teachers' institute."

Fifth and Sixth Grade Classes
March 11, 1943

*****

"We are learning how to play the different notes on the organ."

"All the grades have new health and safety books now except the first grade. Arlen will get his later on."

"This week we took in $1.90 for War Stamps. The preceding week, we took in the same amount."

"Muriel Copp wasn't in school on Tuesday, March 23rd, because she went to the dentist. All the rest have been here this week. Last week we had only two days of school because of the snowstorm."

"We are nearly through with the afghan for the Junior Red Cross. We have six blocks left to crotchet around."

"There is a new way to salute the flag. Instead of raising your hand toward the flag when you say, 'to the flag,' you leave it on your chest while saying the entire pledge. The reason for this change is that when the Germans say, 'Heil Hitler,' they raise their hand, and our former way of saluting reminded some people of this."

"During art period, some of the pupils made booklets for the study of standard pictures and their artists."

Eighth Grade Class
March 26, 1943

*****

"Some teachers had a meeting on Saturday evening at which they finished the afghan which our school has helped work on for the Junior Red Cross. It is now on display in the County Superintendent's office."

"For defense stamps, we took in $2.80 last Wednesday and $1.80 this Wednesday."

251

"There was no school last Thursday and Friday because there was water running over the road both north and south of the schoolhouse. No children could get there without getting wet."

Fifth and Sixth Grade Classes
April 9, 1943

*****

"The War Stamp sale for this week amounted to $2.10. For the preceding week, it was $2.60."

"This week the upper grades have given picture reports. The pictures that were reported on are: 'Dance of the Nymphs' which was painted by Corot - Senora; 'Avenue at Middelharnis' by Hobbema-Bernice; 'The Fog Warning' by Homer - Lois; 'Boy and Rabbit' by Raeburn - James Muzzy; and 'Harp of the Winds' by Martin - Lowell. Miss Halvorson reported on 'Spring' by Corot and 'The Horse Fair' by Rosa Bonheur."

"Some of the pupils in school gave book reports this week also."

"This afternoon there is to be an Easter party at school. The mothers are all invited. Games, contests, and lunch will be enjoyed."

"There has been perfect attendance all week!"

"Miss Halvorson spent the weekend in Grand Forks."

Eighth Grade Class
April 22, 1943

*****

"For defense stamps last week we took in $2.70 and this week $2.50."

"On Friday afternoon, April 30th, the County Line School attended play day at the North Star School. We took along our temperance posters, one which was made by Lois and Bernice Copp and the other by James Muzzy and Lowell Rude. These were the only posters from this section, so they will be entered in the county contest. Lois and Bernice took part in the Minnesota Quiz Contest, and Bernice won third."

Eighth Grade Class
May 7, 1943

*****

"We raked the school yard on Tuesday, May 18th. Just before going home, we burned the grass we'd raked together and roasted marshmallows which Mr. Rude got for us. We used part of the Citizens' League money for them."

"Marlene Kellberg started school on Tuesday afternoon, and she is going to come the rest of the year."

"The school sale for War Stamps this week amounted to $3.70; for the preceding week, it was $2.90. This week we broke our previous record in buying War Stamps!"

Eighth Grade Class
May 21, 1943

1947-48 County Line Herald

(Compiled by Clara Mae Jorde, County Line Teacher)

Favorite Games

My favorite games are: pump pump pull away, prisoner's base, Chinese wall, too deep, cat and mouse, tag, brownies and fairies, send, and hide and go seek. ----- Marilyn Mattson

My favorite games are: pump pump pull away and dodgeball. I like these games because there is much running in them. I also like to play with the ball. ----- Carol Jaennette

Riddles in Geography

This country is very mountainous. Many people come to this country. We get a special kind of cheese from this country. This cheese goes to many other countries. My Uncle Morris was in this country and went skiing down the mountains. ----- Stuart Solem

This country is the most populated country in the world. If you put the people two feet apart, they would go around the world six times. It is important because it has much silk. It also has the highest mountains of the world. ----- Arlen Solem

She is called the "Land of Ten Thousand Lakes." She has many rapids and cascades, and she is not a mountainous country. ----- Shirley Nelson

This country is very mountainous, and she has one city called the "Venice of the North." She has much iron. My capital, which is also a seaport, freezes up during the winter, and then I have to get out of my country through Narvik, Norway. ----- Shirley Nelson

I am an island. My capital is Manila, and this island lies wholly within the tropics. I was very important during the war. I am an independent island. ----- Dorothy Muzzy

The country I am thinking of is the "Pearl of the East." This country is now free. I was under the rule of the British. Our most famous leader was killed last winter. One of the greatest drawbacks to the development of this country is the caste system. The monsoons are very important to this country. ----- Dorothy Muzzy

We are known as the ABC countries of South America. "A" is the most advanced of the ABC countries. She has a good port on the east coast. "B" is a big country, larger than the United States. She has a lot of swamps in the north. In the lowlands, they have a lot of rubber. In the south and east, there are some mountains. There is a song about the capital city. "C" is a long, skinny, mountainous country. From her name, you would think she was a cold country, but it isn't. It would be just as warm as the United States, if it wasn't so mountainous. ----- James Rude

This country has twenty-eight states, two territories, and a federal district. It is shaped something like a horn. Most of the people are partly or wholly native Indian. The rest are white. The people are mostly poor and live in small, unsanitary villages. They speak the Spanish language and trade very extensively with the United States. ----- Muriel Copp

This country has very strange animal life. It is nearly as large as the United States. The native people belong to a tribe called Aborigines and are very primitive in their ways and make their living by hunting and fishing. There are not as many people in this country as there are in New York. Captain John Smith explored this country and an island near here. This country is especially important for the raising of Merino sheep which are the largest wool producing sheep of the world. The only rivers found here are the Murray and the

Darling. The United States government is made up after this country's government. ----- Muriel Copp

This country has a communist form of government. We find the Ural Mountains in this country. It has always been looking for a port that does not freeze over in the winter. This country is divided up into four natural regions. ----- Arlen Solem

I was discovered and conquered by Spain. The man who led the army was very cruel. His name is Pizarro. He took much gold for the officers of Spain. The Spanish king got rich from him. ----- James Rude

I am said to be a great ice box. I am not a land of ice and snow, but wealth and beauty. There was a great gold rush in my country in 1896. I have many forests and mines. Mr. Seward bought me from Russia for $17,200,000 in 1867. I have paid back this amount many times over. ----- James Rude

In this country, the people wear wooden shoes. There is much water. They have windmills. They have many canals, and in the wintertime, their boys and girls can go skating. ----- Philip Jaennette

Special Recognition

Reading - read the most books

Muriel Copp - 15 books and 10 magazines
Philip Jaennette - 19 books
Carol Jaennette - 15 books

Art - paper tearing project

Roger Solem - tearing a picture of a bowl with some apples
James Rude - tearing a picture of a bird (Raven)

Art - coloring project using crayons

>Shirley Nelson - a picture of a crane standing on a rock near the river
>
>Dorothy Muzzy - a picture of a flower garden and a birdhouse

Health - Muriel Copp, James Rude, and Dorothy Muzzy

Neatness - James Rude and Muriel Copp

Best Bulletin Board

>Shirley Nelson
>
>Roger Solem and Muriel Copp tied for second

Attendance for the Year

>Stuart Solem
>
>"Stuart has not missed a day for the last two years. Since he started school, he has only missed one day. Congratulations Stuart."

Attendance for the Last Six Weeks

>We have had perfect attendance from everyone except for two people. Jimmy and Marilyn Mattson missed one day each.

Police - Shirley Nelson and Roger Solem

Bird Reports and Bird Pictures - Stuart Solem and James Rude

Coming In When the Bell Rings – Carol Jaennette and Roger Solem

Keeping His/Her Hair Neatly Combed - James Rude and Muriel Copp

Doing Their Jobs Promptly - James Rude, Roger Solem, and Muriel Copp

Politeness - Muriel Copp, Roger Solem, and Arlen Solem

Best All-around Student - Roger Solem

Changes in our School

There have been many changes in school in the last two years. Miss Jorde bought many things and fixed the schoolhouse very nicely. A new table for classes, a card table for a library corner, and four folding chairs have been added. The old library has been made into two parts. One part for Miss Jorde's books and the other part for a small library. A small library has been made of fruit crates and painted green. Miss Jorde has painted all these things green and yellow. She has also painted the old library and the chairs for the younger ones green and yellow. She bought many pretty pictures to brighten the school room. Miss Jorde brought her flowers to school also. I have probably forgotten some of the things that have changed, but we will all miss these nice things and Miss Jorde next year.   ----- Muriel Copp

Things That We Shall Always Remember

On May 14th, we went to play day. We had races and jumping contests. We had ice cream bars. Richard and Ellen came over on May 5th when we raked our yard. Mrs. Copp came and hauled the banking away. Then we had a wiener roast. Marilyn, Roger, and Carol washed the windows. Roger, Jimmy, Philip, and Stuart hauled grass that the others raked. Miss Jorde, James, Dorothy, Muriel, Arlen, and Shirley raked the yard. Marilyn and Carol picked up the sticks, mud chunks, and pieces of coal. ----- Stuart Solem

Here are a few of the things I liked about the previous school year. One thing is that we have more art in the schoolroom. We have pictures by the most famous artists, and we drew nature scenes. Some of our pictures are on birds and animals. We had to make birds for bird reports in opening exercises. We drew several nature scenes to take to the fair. This is interesting because most of us like nature work. I have to draw a special scene for the fair. Miss Jorde has helped most of us to take an interest in school by playing and reasoning things out with us. We had play day May 14th.

Most of us liked play day because we played all afternoon, and the children got to know each other better. We also learned how to play fairly with others than those from our own school. Miss Jorde has helped the most of any teacher for me to like school. ----- James Rude

I will remember making bird reports and drawing bird pictures. Another thing which was very much fun was paper tearing. I had never done it before, but I enjoyed it immensely. Making bulletin boards was also fun, though I had to hurry to finish them because I've been very busy all year. Making different kinds of artwork, including drawings for the fair, was a lot of fun. Seventh grade arithmetic, prose and poetry, and spelling were my favorite subjects. I will also remember the teacher that gave me these and other things to like.----- Muriel Copp

The most interesting thing that I will always remember is when we were studying about Japan, and how they raise silkworms. When I found out that Japan was just a little island, I was very much surprised. The food that the people give to the silkworms is mostly mulberry leaves. I liked to learn how the dairy farmers sold their milk and cream. People in Japan are dressed differently than the people here in our country. ----- Jimmy Mattson

On Wednesday May 5th, we raked our yard, and I enjoyed it very much. We had play day on May 14th, and there were a lot of children there. We had pop, cake, cookies, ice cream, salad, and pickles for lunch. ----- Marilyn Nelson

I liked to study the countries in geography. I liked to study on the first people who lived on earth. The way they used to eat their meat interested me. Once when a boy was eating meat, he dropped it into the fire. When he got it, he thought it was much better. ----- Philip Jaennette

I liked play day the very best of all. We had to run and throw the ball, but the other side won. We had lots of fun. I played with a girl that I didn't know, and I also played with Marilyn. ----- Carol Jaennette

I remember when we raked the yard because that was when my mother and Robert and Kathryn came. We had our weiner roast, and it was so windy. We little ones pulled the wagons. Philip and I pulled while Richard and Ellen sat in the wagons. We had lots of fun at play day because we played kittenball. ----- Roger Solem

I liked the last year because we got the soccer ball. We can now play dodgeball, which is one of my favorite games. We have played it many times. We have played other ball games too. I hope it will be just as much fun next year. ----- Arlen Solem

I enjoyed Wednesday afternoon, May 5th. First we raked the yard while Stuart, Jimmy, Roger, and Philip hauled the grass away. When we finished raking the yard, since the little children hadn't come yet, we got together and played captain may I and kittenball. When the little children came, we had our weiner roast. The little children that came were: Kathryn Solem, Gaylene Mattson, Robert Rausch, and Richard and Ellen Jorde.   ----- Shirley Nelson

Notes

PROLOGUE

1   John N. Greer, *The History of Education in Minnesota* (Washington DC: Government Printing Office, 1902) 12.

2   Ibid, 14.

3   Ibid, 23.

4   Ibid.

5   Ibid.

6   Ibid, 12.

7   Ibid, 23.

8   Ibid.

9   State Department of Education. *A History of the State Department of Education in Minnesota.*

10   *Marshall County Commissioners' Record*, Book B, 122.

11   *Polk County Commissioners' Record*, Book B, 369.

12   *Red Lake County Commissioners' Record*, Book A, 96.

13   Red Lake County, *School and Town Ledger*, Book A, 25.

14   Bonnie K. Swantek and Bill Dee, eds., *Where Two Rivers Meet: A 100-Year Centennial History of Thief River Falls 1896-1996* (Thief River Falls, Minnesota: *Thief River Falls Times*, 1996), 51.

15   Ibid.

16   Ibid, 52.

CHAPTER 1: THE BIRTH OF COUNTY LINE SCHOOL – DISTRICT 72-219J

17   "The Old Crossing Treaty and Its Sequel," *MNHS Press,* January 8, 1934.

18   *Polk County Commissioners' Record*, Book A, 290.

19   *Marshall County Commissioners' Minutes*, Book A, 108.

20   *Polk County Commissioners' Record*, Book A, 369.

21   J. H. Hay, "Thief River Falls Schools," in *Thief River Falls and Surrounding Territory*, ed. Olaf Huseby (Grand Forks, North Dakota,1908), 20.

22   Ibid.

23   John N. Greer, *The History of Education in Minnesota* (Washington DC: Government Printing Office, 1902) 54.

24   J. H. Hay, "Thief River Falls Schools," in *Thief River Falls and Surrounding Territory*, ed. Olaf Huseby (Grand Forks, North Dakota,1908), 20.

25   Ibid.

26 "Order of Hearing on Petition to Form New School District." *Warren Sheaf*, December 27, 1894, 4.
27 Berg, Harold. Interview by Loiell Dyrud and author. Personal interview. Berg home near Thief River Falls, Minnesota. Summer 1972.
28 Meyer, Louis. Interview by Loiell Dyrud, Alfred Solem, and author. Personal interview. Oakland Park Nursing Home, Thief River Falls, Minnesota. Oct. 8, 1984.
29 *Marshall County Commissioners' Record*, Book B, 122.
30 Ibid.

CHAPTER 2: THE FRED COPP SCHOOL

31 Solem, Alfred. "Fred Copp Family," Excel Township 1884-1984: A Story of the First Hundred Years, eds. Loiell Dyrud et al., (Warren, Minnesota, 1984) 11.
32 Solem, Alfred. "Alfred Solem's Recollections," *Excel Township 1884-1984: A Story of the First Hundred Years,* eds. Loiell Dyrud et al., (Warren, Minnesota, 1984) 141.
33 "Erickson, Lars and Wife, Axelina," *Pioneer Tales: A History of Pennington County*, eds. Pennington County Historical Society. Thief River Falls, Minnesota, (Dallas, 1976) 541.
34 Copp, Muriel. Interview by author. Phone interview. February 11, 2015.
35 Malberg, Georgia. "History of R.L.Muzzy," *Excel Township 1884-1984: A Story of the First Hundred Years*, eds. Loiell Dyrud et al., (Warren, Minnesota, 1984) 18.
36 "Deed Record No. 30," Red Lake County, Book 27, 605.
39 "North of T.R. Falls News." *Warren Sheaf*, June 6, 1912, p. 8

CHAPTER 3: NEIGHBORHOOD QUARREL

41 "Petition for Formation of a New School District," April 9, 1903. Document held by Marshall County Courthouse.
42 "The City." *The Thief River Falls News*, April 9, 1903, 8.
43 "Petition for Formation of a New School District," April 9, 1903. Document held by Marshall County Courthouse.
44 Letter from Fred Copp et al to Red Lake County Board of Commissioners. Document held by Red Lake County Courthouse.
45 "Order Forming New School District," July 14, 1903. Document held by Red Lake County Courthouse.
46 "The City." *The Thief River Falls News*, June 25, 1903, 8.
47 "The City." *The Thief River Falls News*, July 16, 1903, 8.
48 Letter from John L. Finke to Marshall County Board of Commissioners. Document held by Marshall County Courthouse.

49 "Petition for Formation of a New School District," October 6, 1903. Document held by Marshall County Courthouse.

50 Letter from Edmund Franklyn to A. B. Nelson, Marshall County Auditor, November 14, 1903. Document held by Marshall County Courthouse.

51 "Commissioners' Proceedings." *Warren Sheaf*, December 3, 1903, 1.

52 "Annual Meeting of the Board of County Commissioners of Marshall County." *Warren Sheaf*, January 21, 1904, 2.

53 "Order Forming New School District," July 14, 1903. Document held by Red Lake County Courthouse.

54 Red Lake County Commissioners' Record, Book A, 130.

55 *Red Lake County School and Town Ledger*, Book A, 25.

56 Helen Christensen, "Christensen, Carsten and Karen (Larsen)," *Pioneer Tales: A History of Pennington County*, eds. Pennington County Historical Society. Thief River Falls, Minnesota, (Dallas, 1976) 247.

57 "Deed Record No. 7 – Red Lake County," Pennington County Book 43 of Deeds, 138.

CHAPTER 4: SPECIAL EVENTS

58 Amy Meyer, "Smith, Peter and Catherine (Doverspike)," *Pioneer Tales: A History of Pennington County*, eds. Pennington County Historical Society. Thief River Falls, Minnesota, (Dallas, 1976) 281.

59 "The History of the United Methodist Church," *Pioneer Tales: A History of Pennington County*, eds. Pennington County Historical Society. Thief River Falls, Minnesota, (Dallas, 1976) 491.

60 Georgia Malberg, "History of R. L. Muzzy," *Excel Township 1884-1984: A Story of the First Hundred Years*, eds. Loiell Dyrud et al., (Warren, Minnesota, 1984) 18.

61 "North of T. R. Falls." *Warren Sheaf*, June 6, 1912, 8.

62 Author's phone interview, December 16, 2015.

63 Ibid.

64 Rebecca Solem, "Riverside School District No. 84," Excel Township 1884-1984: A Story of the First Hundred Years, eds. Loiell Dyrud et al., (Warren, Minnesota, 1984) 102.

65 Emily Jacobson Johnson, "Jacobson, Thomas C. and Mathilda (Safford)," *Pioneer Tales: A History of Pennington County*, eds. Pennington County Historical Society. Thief River Falls, Minnesota, (Dallas, 1976) 267.

CHAPTER 5: REMEMBRANCES

66 Emily Jacobson Johnson, "Jacobson, Thomas C. and Mathilda (Safford),"
    Pioneer Tales: A History of Pennington County, eds. Pennington County
    Historical Society. Thief River Falls, Minnesota, (Dallas, 1976) 267.]

CHAPTER 7: WAR EFFORTS

67 Mostue, E.A. (1918, February 14). Rural School Notes. *Thief River Falls News
    Press,* 6.
68 "Steiner News." *Warren Sheaf,* March 6, 1918, 7.
69 "County Schools Sell War Savings Stamps." *Warren Sheaf,* March 6, 1918, 1.
70 "The Teachers' Patriotic League." *Warren Sheaf,* September 18, 1918, 1.
71 Minnesota State Department of Education. *Hand Book for Teachers' Patriotic
    League and Little Citizens League* (C. G. Schulz, 1918).
72 Ibid, 136.
73 *County Line Log,* October 16, 1942, 1.
74 *County Line Log,* March 26, 1943, 1.
75 Author's private collection.

CHAPTER 8: CONSOLIDATION

76 State Department of Education. *A History of the State Department of Education
    in Minnesota,* 9.
77 Wayne E. Fuller, *The Old Country School: The Story of Rural Education in the
    Middle West* (The University of Chicago Press, Chicago & London, 1982) 116.
78 *Polk County Commissioners' Record,* Book B, 373-374.
79 State Department of Education. *A History of the State Department of Education
    in Minnesota,* 10.
80 Ibid.
81 School Board Meeting, January 13, 1930, *Superintendent's Report to Board of
    Education, District 18, Thief River Falls, Minnesota,* 1926-1930.
82 Clifford P. Hooker, Van D. Mueller. *The Relationships of School District
    Reorganization to State Aid Distributions Systems, Part I: Patterns of School
    District Organization,* 25.
83 Marshall County School Survey Committee. *Final Report: School District
    Reorganization for Marshall County.* November 1, 1948. "Introduction," 2.
84 Marshall County School Survey Committee. *Final Report: School District
    Reorganization for Marshall County.* November 1, 1948. "High School Tuition
    Policy Changed," 3.
85 Clifford P. Hooker, Van D. Mueller. *The Relationship of School District
    Reorganization to State Aid Distribution Systems, Part I: Patterns of School
    District Organization,* 25.

[86] Mary Drees, "Mrs. Mary Drees: Red Lake County Superintendent of Schools 1947-1967," *The History of Huot School 1892 to 1966*, eds. Robert W. Larson and Karin Larson Hangsleben, (1990) 35-36.

[87] Marshall County School Survey Committee. *Final Report: School District Reorganization for Marshall County*. November 1, 1948. "Proposed Plan of School District Organization," 4.

[88] Marshall County School Survey Committee. *Final Report: School District Reorganization for Marshall County*. November 1, 1948. "Introduction," 2.

[89] "Tentative Recommendations." *Thief River Falls Times*, September 23, 1948, 19.

[90] "Editorials: School Reorganizing." *Thief River Falls Times*, October 21, 1948, 6.

CHAPTER 9: THE DISTRICT ENDS

[91] Marshall County School Survey Committee. *Final Report: School District Reorganization for Marshall County*. November 1, 1948. "High School Tuition Policy Changed," 3.

[92] Ibid.

[93] "County Board Votes 15 Mill School Levy." *Thief River Falls Times*, December 4, 1947, 1.

[94] Regular Meeting, June 12, 1950, *Superintendent's Report to Board of Education, District 18, Thief River Falls, Minnesota, 1950-51.*

[95] Author's private collection.

[96] "Petition for Change of Boundaries, Consolidation, or Annexation of School Districts," February 27, 1951. Document held by Marshall County Courthouse.

[97] *Pennington County Commissioners' Record*, Book 4, 307.

[98] *Marshall County Commissioners' Record*, Volume H, 19.

[99] Special Meeting, March 28, 1951, *Superintendent's Report to Board of Education, District 18, Thief River Falls, Minnesota, 1950-51.*

[100] *Marshall County Commissioners' Record*, Volume H, 20.

[101] *Pennington County Commissioners' Record*, Book 4, 310.

[102] Special Meeting, March 28, 1951, *Superintendent's Report to Board of Education, District 18, Thief River Falls, Minnesota, 1950-51.*

[103] Clifford P. Hooker, Van D. Mueller. *The Relationship of School District Reorganization to State Aid Distribution Systems, Part I: Patterns of School District Organization*, 26.

[104] Laws of Minnesota 1951, chapter 706, section 6, subdivision 1.

[105] *Marshall County Commissioners' Record*, Book H, 25.

[106] *Pennington County Commissioners' Record*, Book 4, 318.

[107] Author's private collection.

[108] "Voters of Enlarged S.D. 18 Asked to Approve $1,200,000 Bonds Nov. 28." *Thief River Falls Times*, November 23, 1955, 1.

[109] "Deed Record No. 86," Pennington County, 477-78.

[110] "School Board OK's Additions to TRF Dist. 18." *Thief River Falls Times*, November 16, 1955, 1.

[111] *Marshall County Commissioners' Record,* Book H, 191.

[112] Special Meeting, November 22, 1955, *Superintendent's Report to Board of Education, District 564, Thief River Falls, Minnesota, 1955-60.*

[113] "School Bonds are Approved by Big Margin." *Thief River Falls Times,* November 30, 1955, 1.

[114] "School Board Asks Bids on 3 School Buses." *Thief River Falls Times,* March 14, 1956, 1.

[115] Clifford P. Hooker, Van D. Mueller. *The Relationship of School District Reorganization to State Aid Distribution Systems, Part I: Patterns of School District Organization,* 25.

[116] State Department of Education. *A History of the State Department of Education in Minnesota,* 10.

[117] Clifford P. Hooker, Van D. Mueller. *The Relationship of School District Reorganization to State Aid Distribution Systems, Part I: Patterns of School District Organization,* 26.

[118] "History of Consolidation." Minnesota House of Representatives House Research Department. http://www.house.leg.state.mn.us/hrd/issinfo/schdistcon.aspx?src=7

APPENDICES

[119] Laws of Minnesota 1877, chapter 74.

[120] Laws of Minnesota 1893, chapter 155, section 1.

[121] Laws of Minnesota 1891, chapter 26, section 2.

[122] "Order of Hearing on Petition to Form New School District." *Warren Sheaf,* December 27, 1894, 4.

[123] "Commissioners' Proceedings." *Warren Sheaf,* January 10, 1895, 4.

[124] Laws of Minnesota 1901, chapter 20, section 1.

[125] Ibid.

[126] Ibid.

[127] "Commissioners' Proceedings." *Warren Sheaf,* Dec 3, 1903, 1.

[128] "Annual Meeting of the Board of County Commissioners of Marshall County." *Warren Sheaf,* January 21, 1904, 2.

[129] *Red Lake County School and Ledger,* Book A, 25.

[130] "Commissioners' Proceedings." *Warren Sheaf,* June 13, 1895, 4.

[131] "Petition of Legal Voter to be Set Off," June 5, 1903. Document held by Marshall County Courthouse.

[132] "Commissioners' Proceedings." *Warren Sheaf,* Oct. 1, 1903, 1.

[133] *Pennington County Commissioners' Record,* Book 4, 87.

[134] *Pennington County Commissioners' Record,* Book 4, 280.

[135] *Marshall County Commissioners' Record,* Book H, 25.

[136] *Pennington County Commissioners' Record,* Book 4, 318.

APPENDICES

[137] Legal Notice, "Order for Hearing on Dissolution of School District," *Thief River Falls Times,*
October 19, 1955, 13.

[138] *Pennington County Commissioners' Record,* Book 4, 504-505.

[139] *Marshall County Commissioners' Record,* Book H, 191.

About the Author

Peter Solem is a lifelong farmer and retired school teacher. He is a graduate of Lincoln High School in Thief River Falls, Minnesota and the University of North Dakota (UND) in Grand Forks, North Dakota. After earning a Bachelor of Science in Education from UND, he taught for many years at the Northwest Area Learning Center in Thief River Falls.

Solem and his wife, Valerie, currently live on the third generation Solem family farm located near Thief River Falls where they raise registered Black Angus cattle. The Solems have three children: Robert, Andrew, and Rebekah. They also have four grandchildren: Madison, Harper, Kellen, and Autumn.

Peter Solem is a co-author of *Excel Township 1884-1984: A Story of the First Hundred Years* and its sequel *Excel Township 1884-1984: A Story of the Next Twenty-Five Years 1985-2009*.